Anorexia Nervosa

About the Authors

Hans-Christoph Friederich, MD, is Head of the Department of Psychosomatic Medicine and Psychotherapy at the University Düsseldorf. His main research interests are the neurobiology and psychotherapy of eating disorders.

Beate Wild, PhD, is a senior scientist whose research mainly focuses on eating disorders, mental comorbidity in older age, and statistical methods.

Stephan Zipfel, MD, is Head of the Department of Psychosomatic Medicine and Psychotherapy at the University Hospital Tübingen. His research focuses on eating disorders, psychooncology, somatic symptom disorder, and research in medical education.

Henning Schauenburg, MD, is a senior physician and scientist in the field of psychotherapy and psychotherapy process research in mental disorders.

Wolfgang Herzog, MD, is Head of the Department of General Internal Medicine and Psychosomatics at the University Hospital Heidelberg. His research mainly focuses on eating disorders, somatic symptom disorder, and health care research.

Anorexia Nervosa

Focal Psychodynamic Psychotherapy

**Hans-Christoph Friederich, Beate Wild,
Stephan Zipfel, Henning Schauenburg,
and Wolfgang Herzog**

In collaboration with Sandra Schild and Miriam Komo-Lang

Library of Congress Cataloging in Publication information for the print version of this book is available via the Library of Congress Marc Database under the Library of Congress Control Number 2018952869

Library and Archives Canada Cataloguing in Publication

Friederich, Hans-Christoph [Anorexia nervosa. English]
    Anorexia nervosa : focal psychodynamic psychotherapy / Hans-Christoph Friederich, Beate Wild, Stephan Zipfel, Henning Schauenburg, and Wolfgang Herzog ; in collaboration with Sandra Schild and Miriam Komo-Lang.
    Translation of: Anorexia nervosa : fokale psychodynamische Psychotherapie.
    Includes bibliographical references. Issued in print and electronic formats.
    ISBN 978-0-88937-554-3 (softcover).--ISBN 978-1-61676-554-5 (PDF).--ISBN 978-1-61334-554-2 (EPUB)
    1. Anorexia nervosa--Handbooks, manuals, etc. 2. Anorexia nervosa--Diagnosis--Handbooks, manuals, etc.
3. Anorexia nervosa--Treatment--Handbooks, manuals, etc. 4. Psychodynamic psychotherapy--Handbooks, manuals, etc.
I. Title. II. Title: Anorexia nervosa. English.

RC552.A5F75 2018   616.85'2620651   C2018-904488-8

                                                  C2018-904489-6

The authors and publisher have made every effort to ensure that the information contained in this text is in accord with the current state of scientific knowledge, recommendations, and practice at the time of publication. In spite of this diligence, errors cannot be completely excluded. Also, due to changing regulations and continuing research, information may become outdated at any point. The authors and publisher disclaim any responsibility for any consequences which may follow from the use of information presented in this book.

Registered trademarks are not noted specifically as such in this publication. The use of descriptive names, registered names, and trademarks does not imply, even in the absence of a specific statement, that such names are exempt from the relevant protective laws and regulations and therefore free for general use.

The cover image is an agency photo depicting models. Use of the photo on this publication does not imply any connection between the content of this publication and any person depicted in the cover image.

The present volume is a translation of Hans-Christoph Friederich, Wolfgang Herzog, Beate Wild, Stephan Zipfel, & Henning Schauenburg, *Anorexia nervosa: Fokale psychodynamische Psychotherapie* (2014, ISBN 978-3-8017-2582-2), published under license from Hogrefe Verlag GmbH & Co. KG, Germany; revised and adapted for the English-speaking market.

English translation by Viola Renner
English editing by Lena Warrington

© 2019 by Hogrefe Publishing
http://www.hogrefe.com

PUBLISHING OFFICES

USA:	Hogrefe Publishing Corporation, 7 Bulfinch Place, Suite 202, Boston, MA 02114 Phone (866) 823-4726, Fax (617) 354-6875; E-mail customerservice@hogrefe.com
EUROPE:	Hogrefe Publishing GmbH, Merkelstr. 3, 37085 Göttingen, Germany Phone +49 551 99950-0, Fax +49 551 99950-111; E-mail publishing@hogrefe.com

SALES & DISTRIBUTION

USA:	Hogrefe Publishing, Customer Services Department, 30 Amberwood Parkway, Ashland, OH 44805 Phone (800) 228-3749, Fax (419) 281-6883; E-mail customerservice@hogrefe.com
UK:	Hogrefe Publishing, c/o Marston Book Services Ltd., 160 Eastern Ave., Milton Park, Abingdon, OX14 4SB, UK Phone +44 1235 465577, Fax +44 1235 465556; E-mail direct.orders@marston.co.uk
EUROPE:	Hogrefe Publishing, Merkelstr. 3, 37085 Göttingen, Germany Phone +49 551 99950-0, Fax +49 551 99950-111; E-mail publishing@hogrefe.com

OTHER OFFICES

CANADA:	Hogrefe Publishing, 660 Eglinton Ave. East, Suite 119-514, Toronto, Ontario, M4G 2K2
SWITZERLAND:	Hogrefe Publishing, Länggass-Strasse 76, 3012 Bern

Hogrefe Publishing
Incorporated and registered in the Commonwealth of Massachusetts, USA, and in Göttingen, Lower Saxony, Germany

Cover image: © KatarzynaBialasiewicz – iStock.com

Printed and bound in Germany

ISBN 978-0-88937-554-3 (print) • ISBN 978-1-61676-554-5 (PDF) • ISBN 978-1-61334-554-2 (EPUB)
http://doi.org/10.1027/00554-000

Foreword

> *"I do not suffer and must then be well."*
> *"Not only does she not sigh for recovery, but she is not*
> *ill pleased with her condition, notwithstanding all the*
> *unpleasantness it is attended with."*
>
> Lasègue (1873/1997, p. 495)

Much of what we know about the perplexing nature of and contradictions in the psychology of anorexia nervosa goes back to Charles Lasègue's careful and nuanced observations above. Based on these, he issued the following stark warning to clinicians:

> "Woe to the physician who, misunderstanding the peril, treats as a fancy without object or duration, an obstinacy which he hopes to vanquish by medicines, friendly advice, or by the still more defective resource, intimidation." (Lasègue, 1873/1997, p. 493)

In other words, never mistake anorexia nervosa for a passing phase that can easily be fixed.

Today, 150 years later, Lasègue's early descriptions are still very pertinent, as anorexia nervosa remains an extremely challenging disorder to treat. Psychological therapy of anorexia nervosa is hard, as the confluence of several factors creates a "perfect storm." Patients themselves present as inexpressive, or even outwardly bland, giving little away on how they feel. Typically they are very attached to their symptoms, minimize or down-play the seriousness of, or outright threat to their life, from their disorder and are highly ambivalent about treatment. In contrast, family members are understandably often extremely vociferous about their concerns and, in their desperation, may helplessly vacillate between bribery and threats to their relative. Clinicians themselves may feel overwhelmed, fearful, or torn between different feelings and courses of action.

This book is the first-ever evidence-based psychodynamic psychotherapy treatment manual for clinicians working with people with anorexia nervosa. It was written by leading experts in brief psychodynamic psychotherapy and in clinical management and research into psychobiology of anorexia nervosa. Based on their rich clinical and research expertise, these authors have modified the psychodynamic treatment approach to tailor it to the characteristics and needs of this challenging patient group.

The efficacy of the manualized disorder-focused treatment approach presented here was confirmed by the multi-centre randomized controlled ANTOP study of outpatient treatments of anorexia nervosa, currently the largest study of its kind. Patients found the approach highly acceptable. The authors are to be congratulated on the development of this novel, evidence-based treatment manual, which constitutes a very useful clinical and research resource.

The present manual is primarily geared towards therapists with a psychodynamic treatment orientation. However, for therapists working with other treatment approaches it constitutes a valuable aid, to help inform about the unique characteristics and paradoxes of this devastating illness. The book opens insights into the preoccupations, anxieties, and broader inner world of patients with anorexia nervosa, which form the basis for the understanding of the specific psychopathology and are crucial for the development of a robust therapeutic relationship. To help decide on the main treatment focus in a given case, the starting point for the treatment is a detailed initial interview, using criteria of the Operationalized Psychodynamic Diagnosis system. Treatment is centred around a specific therapeutic focus and, combined with a particular therapeutic stance, is structured into three therapy phases. These phases are described in detail in the book, through illustrative case stories and examples of intervention strategies and helpful patient–therapist dialog. The manual is a wonderful resource for broadening therapist understanding and behavior in relation to key features of the illness. To address nutritional aspects of anorexia nervosa, a dietetic guidance document is integrated into the manual.

The evidence from the large ANTOP study, supporting the efficacy of this approach, together with the fact that the manual has been road tested by therapists from ten large eating disorder centres across Germany, attests to the practical applicability of this manual. It is hoped that in its current translation the manual will reach a wide readership and thereby broaden options for outpatient treatment of patients with anorexia nervosa in the English-speaking world. In addition, it is hoped that the manual will act as a catalyst for future psychotherapy research.

Taken together, there are many compelling reasons to wish this book wide dissemination and uptake amongst psychotherapists and researchers alike.

Ulrike Schmidt, December 2018
Professor of Eating Disorders, Head of the Department of
Psychological Medicine, Institute of Psychiatry,
Psychology & Neuroscience,
King's College London, UK

Reference

Lasègue, E.-C. (1873/1997). On hysterical anorexia (a). *Obesity Research, 5,* 492–497.

Preface

Anorexia nervosa, unlike any other chronic illness, provokes a wide range of reactions in observers from "sympathetic identification with the affected person, to curiosity and surprise, or even admiration" (Habermas, 1994, p. 14).

Restrictive eating behavior and self-induced extreme underweight are the most obvious distinguishing characteristics of anorexia nervosa. Observed from a psychodynamic vantage point, patients can be seen to be attempting to stabilize their fragile feelings of self-worth, identity, and autonomy, with the key function of triumphing over their powerful feelings of "hunger" and denouncing other primary needs. Interconnected with this are feelings of uniqueness and exceptionality. The self-destructive consequences of their forced attempts at independence are an increasing state of being underweight, which is associated with social isolation and loss of positive interpersonal contacts, and which may lead to premature death. This set of dynamics, for its part, is disconcerting, and causes in turn an intensification of the patient's anorexic symptoms. The disease-related symptom of *restrictive eating behavior* is influenced by constitutional factors (genetic, epigenetic, endocrinological, etc.) and also includes sociocultural aspects.

The treatment of anorexia nervosa is seen as challenging, mostly because of the pronounced difficulty of winning patients over for treatment and having them adhere to a predetermined therapy setting. This is due to the strong fixation patients have on their symptoms (often combined with partial disease denial), which is accompanied by a pronounced avoidance, an extreme need for autonomy, and a strong subjective gratification in the symptoms. This is the reason the basic initial goal of every anorexia nervosa treatment plan is winning the patient over to the therapeutic process. In relation to treatment success, it is preferable that treatment begins in the early stages, especially because the chronic underweight tends to lead, together with psychophysiological adaptation processes, to the perpetuation of the anorexic symptomatology.

According to the national treatment guidelines for eating disorders of the American Psychiatric Association (APA, 2006), the Association of the Medical Societies in Germany (AWMF, 2011), and the UK National Institute for Health and Care Excellence (NICE, 2017), physically stable patients who are not suffering from severe physical or psychological comorbidities should primarily receive outpatient psychotherapeutic treatment. Systematic analysis of the efficacy of such outpatient psychotherapy has recently been intensified. In the context of the promotion of psychotherapy networks in Germany and funded by the German National Ministry for Education and Research between 2006 and 2013, the efficacy of outpatient psychodynamic psychotherapy for the treatment of anorexia nervosa has been closely investigated. In a large, multicenter randomized controlled trial (the Anorexia Nervosa Treatment of Outpatients study, or ANTOP study), evidence from secondary analyses was collected that showed that a manualized and specifically tailored psychodynamic approach could be superior to treatment as usual (i.e., conventional treatments) at 1-year follow-up (see Section 6.2: The ANTOP Study).

Anorexia nervosa is characterized by multiple contradictory behaviors: the pursuit of an ideal autonomy and the wish for security, inner uncertainty and "splendid isolation", the hoarding of food and starving. These *aporia* constitute the fascination of anorexia nervosa and are all part of the challenge of treating this disorder. The goal of this manual is to provide a deeper understanding of the discrepancies in the inner experiential world of patients suffering from anorexia nervosa. At the same time, suggestions are made for disorder-specific adaptations of psychodynamic interventions and of the therapeutic stance. Our suggestions specifically focus on the repertoire of therapeutic behavior in order to expand the range of competences in the treatment of anorexia nervosa patients.

While we were developing this manual, many patients and their families, as well as our colleagues, showed interest in, and helped contribute to, our research. A heartfelt thank you goes out to them. Especially noteworthy has been the work of C. Growther, I. Eisler, and U. Schmidt from the Maudsley Group (Institute of Psychiatry, Kings College London, UK); the work of the members of the workgroup Anorexia Nervosa in generating the German guidelines for eating disorders (under the charge of S. Herpertz), and more specifically, those for anorexia nervosa (under the charge of A. Zeeck); and that of the therapists involved in the ANTOP study, in providing valuable suggestions for the manual during the workshops; as well as the contributions of H. Kächele, A. Sandholz, and T. Grande in sharing their extensive experience as supervisors for psychodynamic therapy in the treatment of anorexia nervosa patients.

This manual was first published in German in April 2014. Due to the considerable international interest in the landmark ANTOP study, published in the journal *Lancet* (Zipfel et al., 2014), we decided to also publish an English translation of the manual. The current book represents a complete revision of the German publication and integrates the published research findings of the ANTOP study to date.

December 2018
Hans-Christoph Friederich
Beate Wild
Stephan Zipfel
Henning Schauenburg
Wolfgang Herzog

Contents

1 Description of the Disorder

1.1 Description

The case studies of the French physician Ernest-Charles Lasègue (using the term *anorexia hysterica*) and of the British physician Sir William Gull (*anorexia nervosa*), both published in 1873, constituted the first detailed descriptions of anorexia nervosa (Gull, 1873; Lasègue, 1873/1997). Both authors emphasized the psychological causes of anorexia nervosa and the missing disease insight and compliance of the affected individuals. Anorexia nervosa was thus the first autonomously defined eating disorder entity. Exaggerated fasting for religious motives had been documented even earlier, with case descriptions of ascetic, fasting saints going back to the 12th century.

The eating disorder anorexia nervosa was first described in 1873

The current use of the term *anorexia nervosa* (translating as "loss of appetite due to a nervous state") is misleading, since affected persons by no means lack appetite. On the contrary, patients suffering from anorexia nervosa of the binge-eating/purging type show fits of repeated overeating, similar to those of bulimic patients. Instead, it is the preemptive intense fear of gaining weight and the associated bodily changes that are the distinguishing symptoms. The *phobia of gaining weight* as the central motive for prolonged fasting was delineated as the core differential diagnostic criterion by the German-American psychoanalytic therapist Hilde Bruch. In her popular book *The Golden Cage: The Enigma of Anorexia Nervosa* (Bruch, 1978), Bruch helped form an awareness and understanding of the disease, not only for doctors and therapists, but also for the general public.

1.2 Definition

The diagnostic criteria of the *International Classification of Mental and Behavioral Disorders* (ICD-10; Chapter VF) of the World

Health Association (WHO, 1992) and of the *Diagnostic and Statistical Manual of Mental Disorders,* fifth edition (DSM-5) of the American Psychiatric Association (APA, 2013), with a few exceptions, show agreement regarding the disorder of the disease anorexia nervosa (see Table 1). A stable version of the 11th revision of the ICD was released on June 18, 2018 for the implementation phase (WHO, 2018). The final version is due to be released in 2022.

Table 1
Diagnostic criteria for anorexia nervosa according to the ICD-10 and DSM-5

DSM-5	ICD-10 (F50.0)
A. Restriction of energy intake relative to requirements, leading to a significantly low body weight in the context of age, sex, developmental trajectory, and physical health. *Significantly low weight* is defined as a weight that is less than minimally normal or, for children and adolescents, less than that minimally expected.	A. Body weight is maintained at least 15% below that expected (either lost or never achieved), or Quetelet's body-mass index (= weight (kg) to be used for age 16 or more) is 17.5 or less. Prepubertal patients may show failure to make the expected weight gain during the period of growth.
B. Intense fear of gaining weight or of becoming fat, or persistent behavior that interferes with weight gain, even though at a significantly low weight.	B. The weight loss is self-induced by avoidance of "fattening foods". One or more of the following may also be present: • self-induced vomiting; • self-induced purging; • excessive exercise; • use of appetite suppressants and/or diuretics.
C. Disturbance in the way in which one's body weight or shape is experienced, undue influence of body weight or shape on self-evaluation, or persistent lack of recognition of the seriousness of the current low body weight.	C. There is body-image distortion in the form of a specific psychopathology whereby a dread of fatness persists as an intrusive, overvalued idea and the patient imposes a low weight threshold on himself or herself.

Table 1 (continued)

DSM-5	ICD-10 (F50.0)
	D. A widespread endocrine disorder involving the hypothalamic – pituitary – gonadal axis is manifest in women as amenorrhoea and in men as a loss of sexual interest and potency. (An apparent exception is the persistence of vaginal bleeds in anorexic women who are receiving replacement hormonal therapy, most commonly taken as a contraceptive pill.) There may also be elevated levels of growth hormone, raised levels of cortisol, changes in the peripheral metabolism of the thyroid hormone, and abnormalities of insulin secretion.
	E. If onset is prepubertal, the sequence of pubertal events is delayed or even arrested (growth ceases; in girls the breasts do not develop and there is a primary amenorrhoea; in boys the genitals remain juvenile). With recovery, puberty is often completed normally, but the menarche is late.
Coding note: The ICD-9-CM code for anorexia nervosa is **307.1,** which is assigned regardless of the subtype. The ICD-10-CM code depends on the subtype (see below).	
Specify whether: **(F50.01) Restricting type:** During the last 3 months, the individual has not engaged in recurrent episodes of binge eating or purging behavior (i.e., self-induced vomiting or the misuse of laxatives, diuretics, or enemas). This subtype describes presentations in which weight loss is accomplished primarily through dieting, fasting, and/or excessive exercise.	

Table 1 (continued)

DSM-5	ICD-10 (F50.0)
(F50.02) Binge-eating/purging type: During the last 3 months, the individual has engaged in recurrent episodes of binge eating or purging behavior (i.e., self-induced vomiting or the misuse of laxatives, diuretics, or enemas).	

Specify if:
In partial remission: After full criteria for anorexia nervosa were previously met, Criterion A (low body weight) has not been met for a sustained period, but either Criterion B or C is still met.

In full remission: After full criteria for anorexia nervosa were previously met, none of the criteria have been met for a sustained period of time.

Specify current severity:
The minimum level of severity is based, for adults, on current body mass index (BMI) (see below) or, for children and adolescents, on BMI percentile. . . . The level of severity may be increased to reflect clinical symptoms, the degree of functional disability, and the need for supervision.
Mild: BMI ≥ 17 kg/m²
Moderate: BMI 16–16.99 kg/m²
Severe: BMI 15–15.99 kg/m²
Extreme: BMI < 15 kg/m²

Both classification systems define the central characteristics of the illness as underweight, a distortion of perceived body shape, and weight phobia. In addition, two subgroups (types) of anorexia patients are differentiated in the DSM-5 and the upcoming ICD-11.

Patients of the ascetic subtype show an extremely restrictive eating behavior, while patients of the binge-eating/purging subtype have, additionally, episodes of binge eating paired with active measures to effect weight loss (such as self-induced vomiting and/or the misuse of laxatives and diuretics). The validity of these subtypes has not been ascertained, because affected individuals often show a transition between the two subtypes. Especially in the first 3 years after onset, a transition from the restrictive to the purging subtype can be observed. To take this dynamic into account, the DSM-5 includes a time frame for dominant symptoms of "the past 3 months" to better differentiate the subtypes.

In comparison to ICD-10 (WHO, 1992), where the weight criteria are defined using a body mass index (BMI) of ≤ 17.5 kg/m^2 in adults and a body weight that falls below the 10th age-percentile in children and adolescents, the ICD-11 weight criterion is defined as a BMI of ≤ 18.5 kg/m^2 in adults (WHO, 2018). In the DSM-5, the weight criterion of the 4th revision (DSM-IV; "< 85% of the minimally expected weight") was repealed and replaced with the definition of "a weight less than minimally normal" (APA, 2013). Thus, the revised weight criteria in the DSM-5 and ICD-11 will include a significantly larger group of adult patients than before.

A further classification criterion of anorexia nervosa appears in the ICD-10, which highlights endocrinological disorders for both women (amenorrhea) and men (loss of libido and/or suffering impotence). In clinical practice, the criterion of amenorrhea is often not determinable, because the use of contraceptives prior to the onset of menstruation by youths and the state of being postmenopausal in older women confound it. Thus, for the DSM-5 and for ICD-11, it was proposed that this criterion should not be included. However, it should be pointed out that anorexia nervosa patients with amenorrhea exhibit a lower bone density and a higher risk for osteoporosis compared with patients with a regular menorrhea.

A further change in the DSM-5 (see Table 1) involves a passage that, in the DSM-IV-TR, suggested a conscious refusal of patients to retain a minimum weight (APA, 2009). This description is suited neither for patients still in the stage of disease denial, nor for those motivated to take part in therapy but who have not managed to gain weight despite their efforts. Depending on the severity and duration

Core symptoms include low weight, distorted perception of body shape, fear of gaining weight

The validity of the definitions of the two subtypes, restrictive and binge/purging type is still unclear

of a patient's extreme low weight, a dysfunctional interaction begins between the physiological and psychological processes that increasingly hinder weight gain and perpetuate anorexic behavior. Appropriately, in the DSM-5 and ICD-11, the focus is on the restricted intake of energy by patients, without the suggestion of conscious or willful behavior. Furthermore, a significant number of patients deny having any fear or phobia of weight gain in their reports. Thus the *phobia of weight gain criterion* was extended to include any behaviors implemented to stabilize low weight, regardless of the patient's emotional motives.

Due to its prognostic relevance, the severity of underweight is also specified. In the DSM-5, a total of four categories, ranging from mild to severe, are differentiated (see Table 1); in the ICD-11, a differentiation is suggested only between patients with significantly low underweight (BMI $\leq$ 18.5 kg/m² and $\geq$ 14.0 kg/m²) and patients with a dangerously low underweight (BMI < 14.0 kg/m²). However, the severity of clinical symptoms, as well as the degree of functional disability, should be included in the evaluation of individual disease severity.

Finally, the DSM-5 criteria allow for the definition of both partial and full remission, after the full criteria have been met (see Table 1).

1.3   Epidemiological and Sociodemographic Data

Anorexia nervosa is a disorder with a prevalence of approximately 0.9% in women and 0.3% in men (Smink, van Hoeken, & Hoek, 2012). However, in chronic cases and in patients receiving treatment, the sex ratio is closer to 10:1 women to men, indicating a shift toward women. Whether or not sociocultural influences (such as slimness mania and diet crazes) have caused an increase in the prevalence of anorexia nervosa continues to be controversial amongst experts. The most recent research based on the DSM-IV definition of anorexia nervosa points mainly to a stable prevalence rate over time (Currin, Schmidt, Treasure, & Jick, 2005; Smink et al., 2012). Moreover, anorexia nervosa is not a disorder that occurs exclusively in Eastern and Western industrialized nations; it is also found in countries in the developing world (Eddy, Hennessey, & Thompson-Brenner, 2007).

The disorder most typically begins in puberty, including late pubertal phase, most commonly between the ages of 11 and 25 (Hudson, Hiripi, Pope, & Kessler, 2007). Thus, anorexia nervosa exhibits a smaller variance for age at onset compared with other eating disorders (such as bulimia nervosa and binge eating), which more often begin at a much older age.

1.4   Predisposing Factors

The predominant risk factors for developing anorexia nervosa are being female and between the ages of 11 and 25 (Jacobi, Hayward, Zwaan, Kraemer, & Agras, 2004). Based on cross-sectional studies, athletes at either recreational or professional levels who take part in aesthetically defined sports (such as gymnastics, ballet, or dance), endurance sports (track and field, triathlon), or weight-dependent sports (such as boxing or wrestling) are also defined as at-risk groups. Prospective studies have shown that young women who are discontent with their body or who participate in a heightened striving for thinness also have a higher risk for developing an eating disorder (Culbert, Racine, & Klump, 2015). To date, evidence that anorexia nervosa is generally on the increase has not been established (Peñas-Lledó, Bulik, Lichtenstein, Larsson, & Baker, 2015).

With reference to personality structures, longitudinal studies found that emotional instability, the dominance of negative affect (neuroticism), and low self-esteem constitute risk factors for developing anorexia nervosa (Bulik et al., 2006; Cervera et al., 2003). In retrospective evaluations, premorbid clustering of anxious or obsessive-compulsive personality traits (Cassin & Ranson, 2005; Lilenfeld, Wonderlich, Riso, Crosby, & Mitchell, 2006), as well as insecure attachment (Jewell et al., 2016), were observed in anorexia nervosa patients. More recently, difficulties in socioemotional processing as well as affect regulation (Caglar-Nazali et al., 2014) and a cognitive style characterized by cognitive inflexibility (Wu et al., 2014) have been shown to be potential risk factors for anorexia nervosa.

The most common premorbid traits are anxious-avoidant, obsessive-compulsive, and neurotic traits

In addition, evidence of increased risk for developing anorexia has been found for prematurely born individuals and for individuals suffering from perinatal complications (Cnattingius, Hultman, Dahl, & Sparen, 1999; Favaro, Tenconi, & Santonastaso, 2006). The biological mechanisms underlying this connection remain unclear. Moreover, unsettled eating behavior (e.g., feeding disorders) and heightened gastrointestinal problems in infancy and childhood also increase the risk of developing anorexia (Kotler, Cohen, Davies, Pine, & Walsh, 2001).

1.5   Course and Prognosis

Anorexia nervosa exhibits a high rate of chronic manifestation; the median duration of the disorder is 5 to 6 years with treatment (Berkam, Lohr, & Bulik, 2007; Herzog, Schellberg, & Deter, 1997). Evidence related to the prognosis of anorexia nervosa, however, is limited only to those particular populations who sought treatment. To date, there are no reliable data for the spontaneous course of anorexia nervosa. Population-based investigations in Scandinavian countries suggest that national health systems do not register approximately 50% of anorexia nervosa cases (Keski-Rahkonen et al., 2007). These purportedly less serious cases, which are not officially registered, show spontaneous remission rates of about 67% after 5 years. Overall, in clinical samples, 50% of anorexia nervosa patients make a full recovery, while 30% show partial recovery, and approximately 20% develop a chronic form of anorexia nervosa coupled with severe physical and psychological complications (Löwe et al., 2001; Steinhausen, 2002). The prognosis for treatment in childhood and adolescence is clearly more favorable than that for when treatment first occurs in adulthood (Brockmeyer, Friederich, & Schmidt, 2017). These findings stress that early treatment is an important prognostic factor for recovery.

Currently, anorexia nervosa accounts for the most common cause of death in young women between the ages of 11 and 25. With a standardized mortality rate of 5.9 in the first 14 years after initial diagnosis (Arcelus, Mitchell, Wales, & Nielsen, 2011), this death rate is 6 times higher than that of the healthy population, when age and sex are accounted for, and approximately 2 or 3 times higher (for schizophrenia and depression, respectively) than in other psychiatric disorders. Aside from medical complications, suicide accounts for 20% of fatalities.

1.6   Differential Diagnoses

The predominant core symptom of anorexia is severe underweight. Through this lens, every disorder that involves a significant loss of weight then becomes a potential differential diagnosis. In the following sections, potential psychological and medical differential diagnoses will each be discussed in greater detail.

1.6.1   Psychological Differential Diagnoses

Depressive Disorders

Depressive episodes are accompanied by a change in appetite and often by weight loss. A depression-related decrease in appetite and body weight coincides with the core depression symptoms of anhedonia, depressed mood, and reduced energy. In comparison, anorexia nervosa–specific symptoms such as "fear of weight gain" do not present or occur in milder forms in depressed patients.

Most frequent differential diagnosis from anorexia is decrease in appetite in depression

Anxiety and Obsessive-Compulsive Disorders

Weight loss can also coincide with anxiety or obsessive-compulsive disorders. Affected individuals reduce their food intake – for example, due to fear of choking or vomiting, or fear of consuming contaminated food. Here the differential diagnoses for anorexia nervosa can be difficult to determine, because anorexia nervosa often occurs comorbidly with both anxiety and obsessive-compulsive disorders.

Paranoid Schizophrenia

Sporadically, patients with paranoid schizophrenia suffer from the delusion that they are being poisoned; in these cases, an extreme reduction in food intake also occurs. The clarification of the differential diagnosis is usually straightforward when productive delusional symptoms are present.

Somatic Symptom Disorder of the Gastrointestinal Tract

In individuals suffering from irritable bowel syndrome, a reduction of food intake can result because of extreme levels of pain. The motivation that drives patients with this syndrome to reduce their food intake is easy to differentiate from anorexic motivations. However, it is important to point out that long-standing anorexia patients often experience discomfort similar to irritable bowel symptoms. Typically, anorexia nervosa patients report that their anorexic behaviors began years before the comorbid irritable bowel symptomatology (Perkins, Keville, Schmidt, & Chalder, 2005).

1.6.2   Medical Differential Diagnoses

Medical screening primarily serves to assess medical risks, rather than clarify differential diagnoses

The diagnosis of anorexia relies mainly on the diagnostic interview and in most cases does not necessitate a detailed physical screening. The physical diagnostic criteria shown in Box 1 primarily serve to differentiate the severity of anorexia nervosa cases and to medically monitor the effects of the patient's significantly low weight rather than support the discovery of hidden medical diseases (Zipfel, Giel, Bulik, Hay, & Schmidt, 2015).

Box 1
Recommendations for medical diagnostic methods

- *Physical examination:* measurements of weight, height, blood pressure, pulse rate, and temperature
- *Blood analysis:* complete blood count, tests for sodium, potassium, magnesium, phosphates, creatinine kinase, creatinine, urea, amylase, thyroid-stimulating hormone, and liver enzymes, and urine analysis
- *Instrumental tests:* electrocardiogram, bone density measurement for patients with amenorrhea > 2 years, and, if specially indicated: chest X-ray, ultrasound of the abdomen, gastroscopy, magnetic resonance imaging of the brain, and/or electroencephalogram

---

Box 2 gives an overview of medical differential diagnoses for anorexia nervosa.

Box 2
Medical differential diagnoses

- Endocrinological causes (e.g., hyperthyreosis)
- Malabsorption syndrome (e.g., celiac disease)
- Chronic inflammatory intestinal disease (e.g., Crohn's disease)
- Tumors and strictures in the gastrointestinal tract
- Infectious cachexia
- Tumor cachexia

1.7   Comorbidity

Anorexia often presents with a variety of other psychiatric disorders, especially anxiety disorders including obsessive-compulsive disorder (60–83%) and depression (31–89%); (Godart et al., 2007; Godart, Flament, Perdereau, & Jeammet, 2002; Kaye, Bulik, Thornton, Barbarich, & Masters, 2004). Generally, it must be taken into account that the symptoms of depression and of obsessive-compulsive disorder can improve when weight has been regained. Inversely, anorexic symptoms can cover up anxiety disorder or posttraumatic stress disorder that first presents when weight gain has been achieved. Anxiety disorders more often precede anorexia than episodes of depression (> 50% of cases), and their occurrence appears to be independent of disease stage of anorexia nervosa (Agras et al., 2004; Godart et al., 2002).

Frequent comorbid disorders with anorexia nervosa are depression and anxiety disorders

Anxiety disorders often precede anorexia and are verifiable, independent of the stage of illness

Furthermore, individuals suffering from anorexia nervosa show a high rate of comorbidity with personality disorders (Cassin & Ranson, 2005; Lilenfeld et al., 2006). With regard to the restrictive type of anorexia, the cluster C personality disorders (anxious-avoidant, obsessive-compulsive, and dependent) are more frequently present. An additional, often observed and striking characteristic is the pursuit of perfectionism and avoidance of mistakes. The avoidance of mistakes shows a high correlation with the presentation of an obsessive-compulsive personality (Egan, Wade, & Shafran, 2011). With regard to other personality constructs, as measured, for example, with the Temperament and Character Inventory (Cloninger, Svrakic, & Przybeck, 1993), anorexia patients score high on *harm avoidance* and *persistence,* while showing low values for *novelty seeking* (Cassin & Ranson, 2005).

Despite intense research, many issues remain unclear: For example, it is unclear to what extent comorbid disorders are the cause or the consequence of anorexia nervosa, or possibly even the result of a common underlying predisposition. Research has proven that psychological comorbidities influence not only treatment success but also the prognosis of anorexia nervosa. In the course of the illness, a mutual relationship between comorbid disorders and anorexia nervosa develops; this should be acknowledged and considered in the course of treatment.

1.8   Diagnostic Instruments and Documentation

Anorexia can often be diagnosed on sight. But in some cases, patients try to hide their abnormally low weight by wearing especially wide clothing or multiple layers of clothing. By measuring body weight, the underweight can be quantified. It should be noted that anorexia nervosa patients may try manipulate their weight by drinking large amounts of fluids or wearing weights under their clothing or in their pockets.

In the presence of abnormally low body weight, the suspicion that anorexia nervosa is present can be validated through focused questioning regarding additional core diagnostic criteria in the course of a structured clinical interview – for example, the Structured Clinical Interview for DSM-5 Disorders (SCID; First, Williams, Karg, & Spitzer, 2016). The particular value of such a structured interview is that it also systematically registers comorbidities. Limitations include the confined spectrum of psychological phenomena that can be registered in the classic systems.

For further diagnosis, specific interviews pertaining to eating disorders are available

For an extended disorder-specific diagnostic interview, guidelines have been developed that assess additional disorder-specific information that is meaningful in the planning stage of treatment.

The most widely utilized expert interview is the Eating Disorder Examination (EDE; Fairburn & Cooper, 1987), an expert interview used internationally. This structured interview focuses on the specific psychopathology of eating disorders, with scales pertaining to *restrained eating, eating concerns,* and *weight, shape concerns.* With the use of 14 additional diagnostic items, together with the criteria of the current DSM, a differentiated classification can be made for anorexia nervosa, bulimia nervosa, and binge-eating disorder. The latest adaptions of the interview to the diagnostic criteria of the 5th edition of DSM can be found on the Centre for Research on Eating Disorders at Oxford (CREDO)   website (http://www.credo-oxford.com/).

There are many self-evaluation tools for eating disorders

In addition, the diagnostic tools that ascertain eating disorders include several self-evaluation questionnaires, so numerous they cannot all be described here. However, two selected questionnaires that have proven to be useful in clinical practice are briefly discussed here. The Eating Disorder Examination–Questionnaire (EDE-Q; Fairburn & Beglin, 2008) is the questionnaire version of the structured expert interview the EDE described in the previous paragraph. Analogous to the EDE, the EDE-Q assesses eating behavior on four subscales that focus on restrictive eating, worries related to eating, weight, and body shape concerns. Additional items have been added that register attacks of binge-eating, self-induced vomiting, and the misuse of diuretics or laxatives.

The Eating Disorder Inventory (EDI; Garner, Olmstead, & Polivy, 1983) focuses on the psychopathology that most commonly accompanies anorexia nervosa and bulimia nervosa. In the most current version (EDI-3; Garner, 2004), 12 primary scales are covered in 91 items: (1) drive for thinness, (2) bulimia, (3) body dissatisfaction, (4) low self-esteem, (5) personal alienation, (6) interpersonal insecurity, (7) interpersonal alienation, (8) interoceptive deficits, (9) emotional dysregulation, (10) perfectionism, (11) asceticism, and (12) maturity fears. The core symptoms of anorexia are registered using the scales (1) drive for thinness, (2) bulimia, and (3) body dissatisfaction (Garner, 2004).

Further diagnostic instruments that can be used to differentiate an eating disorder include the *Practice Guideline for the Treatment of Patients With Eating Disorders* (3rd edition) of the American Psychiatric Association (APA, 2006) and the NICE guidelines for core interventions in the treatment and management of anorexia nervosa, bulimia nervosa, and related eating disorders (NICE, 2017).

Of the diagnostic tools discussed above, the EDI-3 is the most appropriate for assessing those aspects of the disorder that are in line with the psychodynamic understanding of anorexia nervosa. The scales pertaining to interpersonal alienation and insecurity, asceticism, and fears of maturing most closely reflect the psychodynamic framework. However, to date there are no specific psychodynamic assessment tools that can diagnose, or identify the progress markers for, anorexia nervosa.

As a standardized multiaxial diagnostic system for psychodynamically oriented therapists that allows for the delineation of a psychodynamic treatment focus, we recommend the use of a preliminary interview according to the guidelines of the *Operationalized Psychodynamic Diagnosis OPD-2* (Operationalized Psychodynamic Diagnosis Task Force, 2008). A more specific description of this procedure is presented in Chapter 3.

2   Theories and Models

The development and maintenance of anorexia nervosa result, like other psychiatric disorders, from a complex interaction of intrapsychic, sociocultural, familial and biological factors. Evidence for a simple model of disorders that is purely monocausal and relies on a typical family constellation or on a specific genetic defect does not exist.

2.1   Psychodynamic Understanding

The psychodynamic theory of anorexia nervosa makes use of basic psychoanalytical concepts (such as drive psychology, object relations theory, ego psychology, and attachment theory) that have both an intrapsychic and interpersonal focus.

2.1.1   The Intrapsychic Dynamic

From a classical psychoanalytic perspective, the drive theory position of anorexia nervosa has been focused on for an extended period of time. Drive theory proposes that there is a shift from sexual impulses to oral impulses; sexual wishes and physical/genital sexuality are sublimated and denied through starvation. Bodily changes that coincide with sexual maturity, such as secondary sexual characteristics or menstruation, are deflected or delayed. In addition, sexual liaisons rarely exist in the relationships of anorexia patients. The developmental task of achieving independence from the parental home is delayed; the patient "stops time" and becomes an "eternal daughter." In her unconscious fantasies, she can thus remain an "integral object" for both the father and mother.

From its theoretical beginnings, the study of anorexia nervosa often included hints of a *pre-oedipal theme*. Thomae (Thomae, 1963) emphasized the singular importance of the oral phase of the disorder. Patients with anorexia nervosa often describe their mothers as overly protective, intrusive, extremely worried, or focused on appearance and lacking sensitivity for their daughter's needs and wishes. In contrast, they often describe their fathers as being distant, absent, and overly successful professionally, which promotes an ensnared mother–daughter attachment and hinders the daughter's developmental stages for autonomy. The negative representations of both parental figures are associated with the formation of a negative self-image. Anorexia patients remain loyal and hold onto the hidden parental demands by renouncing their own desire for independence (Bers, Besser, Harpaz-Rotem, & Blatt, 2013).

Thus, the struggle for autonomy becomes a central theme based on early experiences of unreliability in primary relationships and a resulting helplessness (Boris, 1984). It is postulated that based on the patient's experiential background, a fear of object loss and loss of self (or even a general loss of control) develops later in life. Normally, during puberty, but also during the early adolescent phase, self-assertion and differentiation from parental figures is a principal developmental task. But with anorexia nervosa, the meaningful experience of testing one's independence from the primary parental figures is avoided. This explains the often observed overly adapted behavior of patients with anorexia nervosa. Those children in particular who become behaviorally assimilated over an extended period of time can experience the disorder as a dysfunctional possibility to avoid new developmental tasks during puberty and, at the same time, unfold the powers of the disorder.

By successfully controlling hunger and weight, self-assertion efficacy is reduced to an intrapsychic and interpersonal experience of control. This involves the defense mechanism of *adolescent asceticism* described by Anna Freud (Midgley, 2013). The conscious renunciation of the pleasures of adolescence serves some individuals as a coping mechanism for age-specific uncertainties and developmental tasks.

The anorexic conceptual life design is a guarantee of emotional safety and control

Through this lens, typical trigger situations such as a real or fantasized separation from the parental home (e.g., graduating from school, student exchanges, working as an au pair, moving into one's first apartment) or age-specific uncertainties caused by first erotic adventures or disappointments can be better understood. During adolescence the anorexic conceptual life design has an identity-building function that conveys emotional safety and control.

In the preliminary phase of treatment, the hazards of starvation and its self-destructive effects are vehemently denied by patients. From disease onset, an aspect of self-destructiveness emerges that can be understood as a hidden expression of aggressive impulses, or as hidden feelings of desire or greed. These impulses are experienced as forbidden and threatening, which is why they are repressed into the defense mechanism of masochistic self-punishment. Purging behavior, and especially self-induced vomiting, is conceptualized as the patient's defense mechanism to undo something. Patients express their negative self-perception and self-criticism with an extreme discontent with their body.

As anorexia nervosa progresses, symptoms (such as a continuous preoccupation with food, coupled with an intense attentiveness to food-associated stimuli) develop that can be understood in hunger–physiological terms. These cognitive phenomena and behaviors were shown, for example, in healthy males in the course of experiments focusing on hunger mechanisms (Keys, Brozek, Henschel, Mickelsen, & Taylor, 1950). Additionally, it appears that neurobiological alterations caused by starvation promote the perpetuation of extreme underweight.

2.1.2　The Interpersonal Dynamic

The relationship patterns of patients with anorexia nervosa are characterized by an anxious-avoidant attachment style (Ward, Ramsay, Turnbull, Benedettini, & Treasure, 2000). The anxious attachment style correlates to early experiences of rejection and a controlled, distanced style of interaction of the primary parental caregivers (Bartholomew, Kwong, & Hart, 2001). Based on these experiences with important caregivers, internal representations develop that combine a negative self-representation (insecurity, inferiority, dependence, and helplessness) and a negative representation of others (critical, dominant, uncaring, or overly caring). By avoiding intimacy in relationships, patients' painful early memories are repressed. To ward off the perceived threatening dependence on others, patients with anorexia nervosa establish narcissistic ideals of autonomy and autarky ("I need no one and am content to be alone"; Brockmeyer, Grosse Holtforth, Bents, Herzog, & Friederich, 2013). This superficial avoidant relationship pattern and the fight for independence is, to a high degree, associated with self-worth gratification, albeit at the cost of positive interpersonal experiences. In terms of primary human needs, the successful denial of food intake becomes an important resource for the narcissistic feelings of uniqueness, outstanding quality, and independence. By means of this anorexic conceptual life design, patients separate themselves from their family, and at the same time prevent the physical separation from the parental home through the disorder.

Also, dependence on others is often expressed by self-sacrificing caregiving for others. The conceptual life design of anorexia patients establishes a dysfunctional compromise between extreme object-loss anxiety and the pursuit of autonomy.

The avoidance of interpersonal conflicts, together with the socially distanced relationship offers made by patients with anorexia nervosa, are associated with a limited emotional competence that hinders the emotional processing of traumatic situations of loss (Brockmeyer et al., 2012). Furthermore, it seems that patients, particularly those in an extreme state of weight loss, have only limited access to autobiographical memories that are emotionally relevant, including conflicting relationship themes (Brockmeyer et al., 2013).

Box 3 and Figure 1 summarize typical intra-psychic and interpersonal aspects of anorexic behavior.

Box 3
Typical intrapsychic and interpersonal aspects of anorexia nervosa behavior

- A lonely, distanced form of relationships is preferred. Although painful for the affected parties, it reduces the risk of confronting problems of self-worth.
- Needs are repressed, as they are experienced as synonymous with a loss of self-control.
- Extreme weight loss and starvation reduce interpersonal feelings, especially in relation to the opposite sex. These symptoms express emotions and attitudes without the need for openly speaking about them. A gain in weight would mean embracing and accepting life and its developmental tasks, including the role of being female.
- Hunger is often experienced as self-punishment, perceived as being deserved for being a "bad person," or as punishment for an insatiable appetite and craving for food, or for the patient's preoccupation with weight and body shape.
- The patient with anorexia nervosa wishes to be unique and independent and yet remain a "child." The malnutrition and low weight are meant to illicit caring behavior from others.
- Anorexic behavior expresses an unconscious indictment of family, environment, therapist, etc., without which the patient would be culpable (as she is ill).
- The eating disorder serves to repress any depressive mood, which is strengthened by social isolation and the exhaustion of intrapsychic processes.

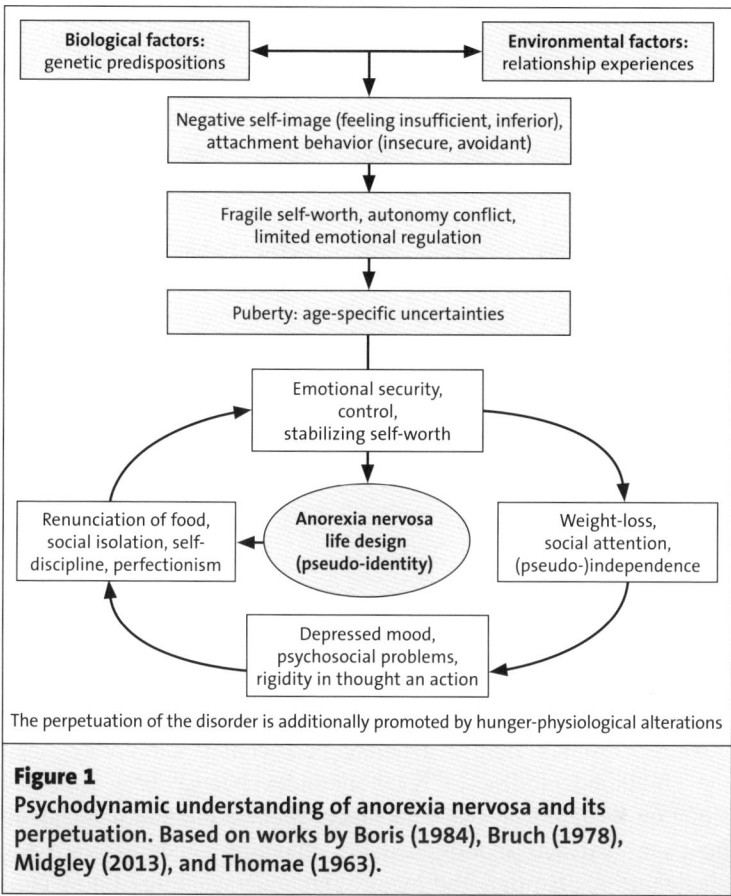

Figure 1
Psychodynamic understanding of anorexia nervosa and its
perpetuation. Based on works by Boris (1984), Bruch (1978),
Midgley (2013), and Thomae (1963).

2.2   Concepts of the Cognitive Behavior Theory Model

The cognitive behavior therapy (CBT) model postulates that dysfunctional beliefs relating to food, figure, and weight play a central role in the emergence and maintenance of anorexia nervosa (Garner & Bemis, 1982). Patients with anorexia nervosa are overly concerned with their weight and shape, and overly focused on weight control. Furthermore, the cognitive model argues that patients' feelings of self-worth are exclusively regulated by satisfaction with their weight and shape ("I only have value when I am thin"). On the behavioral level, patients attempt to control these three areas with a strict diet, daily weighing, and control of their figure (e.g.,

In CBT, maladaptive thoughts and behaviors applied to eating, body shape, and weight play a pivotal role wearing specific pants or belts). The restrictive eating behavior and the resulting weight loss lead to a multitude of biological and psychological changes that perpetuate, in a vicious circle, the anorexia nervosa disorder. As seen in the restrictive type of anorexia nervosa, the restrained eating behavior and the increasingly bloated feeling during food intake reinforce the selective attentiveness to food, figure, and weight and the control thereof. For the binge-eating/purging type of anorexia nervosa, the dynamic is caused by the restrained eating behavior, which triggers binge-eating and its compensatory measures. The fear of gaining weight that is caused by the binge-eating attacks, in turn reinforces restrained eating practices (Fairburn, 2008). The most recent literature in behavioral therapy integrates the fields of psychodynamic origins, such as the development of autonomy/individuation, the conflicts of sexuality, and the problems of self-worth (Fairburn, 2008).

2.3   Family Dynamic Aspects

Since the adolescent process of detachment develops in the context of family relationships, the entire family is affected by the anorexic disorder. From a family dynamic perspective, adolescence and the childhood process of reaching independence is a threshold situation for families. The detachment process of adolescents, with their ambivalence, moods, and fast-changing needs, poses many challenges for families and requires an understanding of how individual family members (and the family as a whole) will reorganize themselves in the eventual absence of the detached adolescent. An important framework for their child's detachment process is based on the parents' experiences of their own personal detachment (or nondetachment) – experiences that in this context include their successes, failures, and fears, as well as perceptions of their own future as a couple.

A delay in the adolescent task of detachment encompasses the complete family system

Including family members in family session treatment is extremely important, especially for younger patients (Herzog, Kronmüller, Hartmann, Bergmann, & Kröger, 2000; NICE, 2017). From a family dynamic viewpoint, anorexic behavior is a dysfunctional attempt at solving interpersonal conflicts within the family (Selvini-Palazzoli, 1996). By way of the clinical appearance of anorexia nervosa, the "adolescent anorectic distinguishes herself from her family without having to separate from them" and "rebels against her parents without having feelings of guilt," because she is sick and suffering (Reich, Cierpka, & Becker, 2010, p. 138). The body becomes an instrument of communication in the relationship between the child and the parents.

2.4 Sociocultural Aspects

In the context of rapidly increasing rates of obesity in industrialized countries, considerable sociocultural pressure has arisen for girls and young women to adhere to beauty and slimness ideals that cannot be met with normal eating behavior. Over the past decades, documentation of the decreasing weight of beauty pageant winners; the eating disorders of supermodels; and the descriptions of the *female athletes' triad*" (i.e., eating disorder, amenorrhea, and osteoporosis) shows the emergence of a mosaic of components reflecting slimness ideals.

> Sociocultural aspects have more significance as a trigger than as a cause of anorexia nervosa

Over the past 50 years, the incidence rate of anorexia nervosa has stabilized. In all likelihood, sociocultural pressures have played a key role in causing the other eating disorders (bulimia nervosa, binge-eating disorder, etc.); in anorexia nervosa, however, these pressures influence specific aspects of the phenomenology of the disorder without actually causing it. Due to deficiencies in self-confidence, patients with anorexia nervosa often use social comparisons to regulate and stabilize their self-worth (Troop, Allan, Treasure, & Katzman, 2003). In these comparisons, a focus is placed on appearance as well as shape.

2.5 Biological Aspects

Apart from the concept that anorexia nervosa is a psychosocially influenced disorder, awareness is increasing regarding the specific neurobiological vulnerabilities that substantially contribute to the emergence and maintenance of anorexia nervosa.

> In the emergence and maintenance of anorexia nervosa, biological aspects are also relevant

Twin research points to molecular biological components that are of importance in the emergence of anorexia nervosa: Identical twins show a higher concordance for anorexia nervosa than fraternal twins. While a molecular-genetic predisposition for anorexia nervosa is estimated at between 48% and 74% in population genetic studies, the exact mechanisms of heredity transmission are not yet known (Bulik, Kleiman, & Yilmaz, 2016). To date, the largest genome-wide association study (of 3,500 patients) found a significant genome-wide locus on chromosome 12 in a region related to metabolic and autoimmune disorders (Duncan et al., 2017). In addition to negative correlations between anorexia nervosa and metabolic traits, significant positive genetic correlations were observed between anorexia nervosa and other psychiatric disorders. This suggests that anorexia nervosa is not only a mental but also a metabolic disorder (Duncan et al., 2017).

Neurobiologically, anorexia nervosa is conceptualized as a neurodevelopmental disorder. The typical onset of the disorder is in adolescence, a phase accompanied by intensive brain maturation that is influenced by hormonal changes. Neurobiological research has proven that alterations in limbic and frontostriatal networks exist that play a role in self-regulation and motivation (Friederich et al., 2012; Friederich, Wu, Simon, & Herzog, 2013; Zastrow et al., 2009). Studies in developmental-psychology also show that age-dependent maturation in the frontostriatal and limbic systems strongly coincides with the development of self-regulatory and motivational factors. Furthermore, there is growing evidence to support neurobiological progression with poorer outcomes once the illness exceeds several years in duration (Schmidt, Brown, McClelland, Glennon, & Mountford, 2016).

Studies of the neurotransmitters in the dopamine and serotonin systems support the change in responsiveness of the neural networks involved in self-regulatory control (i.e., shift to compulsive and habitual behaviors) as well as reward processing (Kaye, Fudge, & Paulus, 2009; Zipfel et al., 2015). These neural changes are associated with cognitive-motivational impairments that can result – for example, in a heightened rigidity in thinking and behavior, or in a change in reward sensitivity.

It is unclear whether or not observed neurobiological changes are causes or the result of anorexia nervosa

Current studies have been conducted exclusively on acute cases or weight-remitted patients suffering from anorexia nervosa. Thus, it remains unclear whether or not the observed changes in neurotransmitters are of etiological importance or if the changes emerge exclusively during a state of extreme low weight as a consequence of long-lasting underweight (*scar effect*). Severe underweight causes a 20% atrophy of brain volume, especially of gray matter. This change in volume appears to be largely reversible with weight restoration, though a permanent neural impairment cannot be ruled out (Friederich et al., 2012). To show whether or not these changes are present as trait markers at disease onset, future studies are needed that take a prospective approach by assessing young women who are at risk of disease.

3 Diagnosis

The basic concept of focal psychodynamic short-term therapy, when applied to patients with anorexia nervosa, is the focused treatment of a specific therapy theme (i.e., the focus), which is described in relationship dynamic terms and considers not only central conflict themes, but also structural weaknesses. This focus-oriented therapy requires thorough and precise psychodynamic diagnostics. The authors recommend using the interview guidelines of the OPD-2 (see Section 3.1: Operationalized Psychodynamic Diagnosis). This approach ensures that the central psychodynamic aspects of the patient's disorder are the main focus of treatment. In this sense, the therapy focus becomes an integrating and behavior-governing function that underlies the therapeutic process.

3.1 Operationalized Psychodynamic Diagnosis

Operationalized psychodynamic diagnosis (OPD-2; OPD Task Force, 2008), as a system of reference, allows for a comprehensive personality-based diagnosis of the *patient's disease experience* (Axis I); typical maladaptive *interpersonal relations* (Axis II); and life-determining, dysfunctional *conflicts* (Axis III); as well as resources and deficits in structural psychological *ego functions* (Axis IV).

The OPD-2 can be used to guide therapy

The OPD approach is psychodynamic. This means that aspects of repressed or defended motives and feelings, as well as the reenactment of early relationship experiences in the current therapeutic process (transference and countertransference), are taken into account. These aspects are gathered in the course of a *spontaneous* conversation, while the exploration of the patient follows the manual guidelines that include the following multiaxial approach.

3.1.1   Axis I: Experience of Illness and Prerequisites for Treatment

With regard to Axis I, it is important to note whether or not the patient has a medical or psychosocial understanding of their illness, what their preconceived expectations of the therapy are, what the available resources are, and any potential barriers that exist for the therapy.

3.1.2   Axis II: Interpersonal Relations

In diagnosing the patient's relationship patterns, the focus should be on their unique style of interaction not only in their contacts with the therapist, but also in other relationships. This is based on the exploration of the following interactions: How does the patient regulate their needs? What expectations do they have that underlie their actions? How are conflicts managed? In this analysis, non-verbal elements, as well as the patient's perspective as compared with that of the people they interact with (in this specific case, the interviewers), play an important role.

3.1.3   Axis III: Conflicts

Developments in an individual's life story and personality structures account for a specific conflict disposition that includes an individual pattern of experience and behavior. These patterns include wishes, drives, expectations for the future, assumptions, and experiences. If these patterns become life-determining and dysfunctional, they are defined in the OPD as *life-long conflict themes*. The individual conflict dynamic should be determined on this axis – for example, their general intimacy with or detachment from others, the importance of control in their relationships, the potential for experiencing connectedness and security, or conflicts related to self-worth in general and in connection to personal identity.

3.1.4   Axis IV: Structure

An individual's personality structure comprises their relatively stable pattern of abilities and their deficits when interacting at an intrapersonal and interpersonal level. Included in the diagnosis of an individual's personality structure are the so-called *ego functions*; these ego functions include the ability to perceive oneself and others, to reflect upon inner processes, and the perception, allocation, regulation, and communication of affects. In the OPD, the various structure levels (high, moderate, and low level of structural integration or disintegration) are differentiated based on the quality and availability of these interaction skills.

3.2   Initial Interview and Deriving a Focus for Therapy

An OPD interview should identify the symptomatic, maladaptive relationship patterns, central life-determining conflict themes, and structural deficits of the patient. Based on the interview according to the OPD guidelines, the significant psychodynamic foci of each patient can be determined. The treatment's relevant foci are those characteristics determined by the OPD findings that cause and/or perpetuate the disorder. It is assumed that progress in therapy can only take place if some aspects of the foci are changed. The correct use of the interview guidelines and clinical assessment of patients in accordance with OPD criteria requires completion of training seminars.

To understand the central foci of therapy, the following synopsis of the components of the interview can be helpful.

Clinical Pearl
Elements of the diagnostic interview according to OPD guidelines

1. Symptoms and their severity and chronicity, and comorbidities
2. Symptom presentation, the degree of illness denial and subjective suffering, as well as social and personal resources
3. Distinguishing central interaction partners, and patterns underlying these relationships:
   - Description of parental figures and changes over the years, central conflicts with parental figures
   - Important sibling and peer relationships, personal role in the peer group
   - Relationship experiences, and fears and wishes for romantic relationships and friendships
4. Central conflict themes:
   - Most frequently experienced: need for care versus self-sufficiency, submission versus control, and occasional individuation versus dependency

- Dealing with detachment situations
- Dealing with loss, death, and illness
- Dealing with aggression, and self-assertion
- Deportment when seeking help

5. Important structural features:
   - Self-perception, self-worth (What kind of a person are you? How much appreciation do you have for yourself?)
   - Object perception (through the depiction of important caregivers – see above)
   - Affect differentiation (the experience of aggressive and affectionate impulses, and tensions – see above)

Based on OPD Task Force (2008).

3.3　Operationalized Psychodynamic Diagnosis of Anorexia Nervosa

In the following sections, examples of typical anorexic relationship patterns, most common life-determining conflicts, and most frequent structural foci are provided. In each treatment plan, specific patterns, conflicts, and foci should be chosen for the therapeutic work. A selection should be made that includes central relationship themes and especially important structural impairments. Defining a focus is particularly useful in the middle phase of therapy; therapists should regularly verify if the identified focus interactions are being processed during sessions.

3.3.1　Relationship Patterns

In Box 4, two descriptions of some relationship dynamics are quoted in the words of patients.

Box 4
Descriptions of typical relationship dynamics according to OPD-2

Description 1. I feel controlled by others and yet abandoned. I react to this feeling, on the one hand, by caring for and tending to the needs of others and, on the other hand, by withdrawing from relationships and by demonstrating independence particularly in relation to eating and controlling weight. Others experience me as being controlling and withdrawn. They then react to me in a combination of caring for me, but also by controlling me or withdrawing from me. I experience their behavior as domineering at times and at other times as abandonment.

Description 2. Anorexia nervosa helps me establish a border between myself and others without having to separate myself from them. This is important to me because I experience others as being particularly dominating, while at the same time I harbor an intense fear of possibly losing them. Therefore, I express my need for care with my skinniness. However, when someone cares for me, I react by feeling guilty and withdrawal.

In both these situations, if others then intensify their care giving, it puts more pressure on the patient. At the same time, others may react with self-blame, which increases the patient's guilt and self-deprecation.

Translated and reprinted with permission from *Fokale Psychodynamische Psychotherapie der Anorexia nervosa* [Focal psychodynamic psychotherapy of anorexia nervosa], by H. Schauenburg, H.-C. Friederich, B. Wild, S. Zipfel, and W. Herzog, 2009, *Psychotherapeut*, *54*(4), pp. 272–273, © 2009 by Springer Medizin Verlag.

3.3.2 Topics of Conflict

Frequent central conflict themes are the need for care versus self-sufficiency, control versus submission, and to a lesser extent, that between individuation versus dependency. The last is often associated with structural limitations (OPD Task Force, 2008).

> **Frequent conflicts are the need for care vs. self-sufficiency, and submission vs. control**

The following clinical vignettes illustrate the main conflict themes: the need for care versus self-sufficiency conflict (Clinical Vignette 1), the submission versus control conflict (Clinical Vignette 2), and the individuation versus dependency conflict (Clinical Vignette 3). These case studies are abbreviated to bring out their underlying phenomenological conflicts.

> **Clinical Vignette 1**
> **The "good daughter": Need for care versus self-sufficiency conflict, with a mixed but active mode**
>
> Ms. U. (age 19) has been suffering from an eating disorder of the predominantly restrictive type for the past 3 years. Her body weight at treatment onset was 36 kg, with a height of 155 cm (BMI 15 kg/m²). She is currently in the 11th grade and lives with her parents. Ms. U. describes herself as very agitated and unsettled – for example, when she watches television she constantly performs gymnastic exercises, and she undertakes sports several hours per day.

> **The lead affect in Vignette 1 is worry about others in order to repress feelings of depression**

She plans her day "very tightly." She studies a lot for school, gives tutorials, helps her mother with housework and grocery shopping, volunteers at church, etc. She "cannot allow herself any breaks" and feels overburdened and under pressure. She is the youngest child in her family, with two older brothers and an older sister. Her parents belong to a conservative congregation and the atmosphere at home is strongly affected by her parents' religious beliefs. The convictions and principles of the church have a strong influence on family life (clothing, social contacts, and the role of women). Religious sternness dominates, without real emotional contact between family members. Her parents are very unsettled by her illness and are at a loss for words.

Her mother, who is a homebody and unemployed, "monitors" the inner-family processes. She violates boundaries, and constantly stands in the daughter's room. Until just recently, Ms. U. was not even allowed to close the door to her bedroom.

Her father, who is often away on business, is "more independent and reasonable than mother." He thinks highly of achievement and is proud of his daughter's good grades and ambition. Her siblings moved out long ago. Ms. U. has the notion that as the youngest, she needs to "hold everything together" and live up to her parents' expectations; she therefore involves herself at church. Her siblings broke with the parents' expectations long ago. Ms. U. reports a constant anxiety to please others (parents, peers at school, friends, siblings). She has never had a close relationship with a young man and has never dated. Her parents had forbidden sexual activity while she was under the age of 18. She has never attempted to have a romantic relationship, out of fear that her parents would break ties with her.

The lead affect in Vignette 2 is defiant aggression	**Clinical Vignette 2** **Professional goal: Criminal court judge – Control versus submission conflict, with an active mode**

Ms. F. (age 24) comes to treatment because of a 3-year persisting anorexia nervosa (BMI 15 kg/m^2) of the purging type (excessive sports, misuse of laxatives) and isolated impulse breakthroughs with binge-eating attacks. She denies using self-induced vomiting as weight control. Three years ago, the trigger for her anorexic development was the separation from her boyfriend (same-aged young man) after a 1.5-year steady relationship. She initiated the separation from her boyfriend because she had sensed an extreme "clinginess" and could not bear the closeness. An exacerbation of her symptoms occurred while she was studying for her exams at university. Her career goal is to become a criminal defense lawyer or a criminal judge. She reports a pronounced behavior of controlling weight and figure. She weighs herself about 30 times per day and uses every opportunity to look at her figure in either mirrors or display windows. She describes herself as extremely ambitious and achievement oriented.

In the interaction with Ms. F., a power struggle becomes very clear in the course of the first discussions about the basic conditions of therapy and first goal agreements: "You cannot give me an ultimatum; I will fight against that with everything in my power." She experiences the therapy contract as an external regulation and reacts to the fantasized forfeit of power with defiant aggression in ripping up the therapy contract in front of her therapist or, at times, remaining silent for an entire session. As soon as she feels as though her self-determination is in anyway compromised in any contact with others, she begins devaluating and hurting them. Any kind of weakness, fear, or distress is fought off by the patient by any means possible.

Clinical Vignette 3
The "unapproachable beauty": Individuation versus dependency conflict, with an active mode

Ms. B. (age 19) has suffered from anorexia nervosa for the past 6 years. She is a beautiful young woman with wide eyes. The critical development (BMI 15 kg/m^2) was, in part, brought about by her mother's cancer diagnosis (metastasis of breast cancer), and was intensified because of the increasingly close relationship to her boyfriend (e.g., plans for moving in together).

Ms. B. reports growing up as the middle child between two "here-I-am" personality siblings. She never made much of a fuss over herself. Her father was a "strict patriarch," with whom her siblings often quarreled. She herself entertained a rational, unemotional relationship to him. She reported having a closer relationship to her mother. In spite of her mother's relationship offers and encouragement to open up, the patient reported preferring to keep her mother at bay. The first manifestation of her mother's breast cancer was seen by the patient as a dramatic and far-reaching experience when she was only 12 years old.

Ms. B. always viewed independence as an important quality. At only 13 years of age she went on a student exchange program; when she was 17 years old she joined a group that took a bike tour through America. She is currently repeating Grade 12, but her graduation is again in jeopardy.

For the past 2 years she has been living in a romantic relationship with a "complicated" man 13 years older than her (abuse of alcohol, unemployed, lives with his mother). Their attempt at living together led to extreme quarreling, to the point that she moved back in with her parents. While living with her boyfriend, she experienced his every departure as abandonment.

The lead affect in Vignette 3 is existential fear of closeness, and of merging

3.3.3   Structural Impairments

Apart from the aforementioned conflicting motivational tensions seen in patients with anorexia nervosa, basic limitations of psychological functioning also play a decisive role. These either develop early on (influenced by child–parent relationships) or emerge during the progression of the disorder when caused by psychological developmental delays. The following list describes the typical impairments of the psychological structure of anorexia nervosa patients, such as problems they experience regarding managing both the self and the objects:

1. *Experience of affect and affect differentiation:* Based on their chronic avoidance of affect, patients with anorexia nervosa are often incapable of discerning their inner experience or differentiating between varying feelings (e.g., fear, anger, mourning, boredom, aversion).
2. *Impulse control:* Patients often experience their own affective impulses as being "bad": They criticize and deplore themselves for having such drives and concentrate on either suppressing or transferring their affects into physical activity.
3. *Self-worth regulation:* A high level of taking offense persists, which is expressed through self-depreciation or quick social withdrawal.
4. *Body-self:* The emotional perception of the body is more or less distorted (body image disorder) and accompanied by uncertainty and self-deprecation.
5. *Accepting help:* In spite of a heightened level of neediness, many patients are unable to ask for or accept help from others. The tendency to make excessive demands on oneself persists.
6. *Detaching from relationships:* Through subliminal object dependence (despite a superficial autonomy), patients have difficulty completing important detachment processes from primary caregivers (not only from the mother, but often from the father as well).

3.4   Therapeutic Handling of the Focus

The aforementioned foci offer various approaches on which to base psychotherapy. Relationship patterns allow for the exploration of subjective perceptions of conflict-ridden situations ("What exactly did you experience in this argument with your mother?"). The possibility to expand the patient's perception to an understanding of the perspective of significant others arises. ("What do you think your parents are feeling, when you so devotedly cook for them?"). Conflict themes can be addressed in a manner that promotes the focus on defense mechanisms ("What is of special importance in your life? How do you act toward others when you are feeling ashamed?").

Structural impairments can be explored and alleviated ("If I tried to put myself in your shoes, I think I would feel lonely in this situation. Is it possible that you are afraid of rejection, and would you like to ask for support? What would be helpful for you in gaining a more realistic concept of your body?").

Since patients construct and shape their relationships along the lines of their disorder, we suggest describing the therapy focus in terms of the anorexic symptoms. The focus should be formulated in such a way that it connects the specific pathology of eating behavior with the often unconscious conflicting themes and interactions. During the entire therapy process, but especially near the beginning, changes in weight or in eating behavior should be viewed in relationship to the effects on, and importance for, both the patient and their psychosocial environment. The therapeutic approach should be centered on the three-pronged aspects comprising interpersonal problems, eating behavior and body perception, and associated affects (see Figure 2).

The treatment focus should include the pathological eating behavior

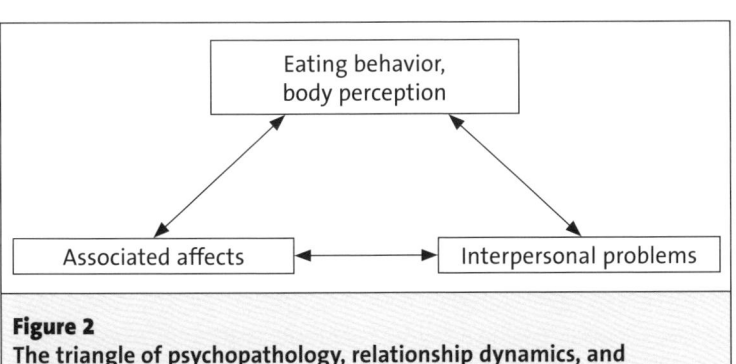

Figure 2
The triangle of psychopathology, relationship dynamics, and associated affects.

In addition to the effect that the disorder has on the relationship structure between patients and parents or other caregivers, particular attention should be paid to the interrelationship between the development of the eating behavior and the formation of the therapeutic relationship. In this sense, it is often sufficient and more effective to use situational examples from the here-and-now, and to allude to parallels with earlier experiences or specific examples from the past.

Intervention Examples

Therapist: How did those in your surrounding environment, your parents, or your siblings react to your weight loss?

Therapist: What does the refusal of food mean for you?

Therapist: How would your parents react to further weight loss? What would they say?

Therapist: Do you see any similarities between your relationship to your parents and our client–therapist relationship? Can you describe these parallels?

4 Treatment

4.1 Treatment Setting

This manual presents the outpatient focal psychodynamic approach of psychotherapy for anorexia nervosa. It was conceived for the randomized controlled German ANTOP study described in Section 6.2, in order to operate within its framework. The length of treatment in this manual has been adapted to the number of outpatient sessions covered by health insurance in Germany – that is, roughly 40–50 sessions. An extension is indicated if the severity or duration of illness warrants it; this would prolong the treatment to a maximum of 100 sessions.

To establish the therapeutic relationship, it is recommended that 2 sessions be offered in the course of the first 2 months. From the third to ninth month of treatment, weekly sessions are required. During the closure phase, the session frequency should be reduced to one session every 2 weeks – which is to counteract the challenges that the anorexic psychodynamic places on the completion of the client–therapist relationship.

4.2 Therapeutic Framework

In both the inpatient and outpatient setting, a therapeutic framework with clear-cut treatment agreements sets the stage for success. The framework imparts security and supports weight gain. It also facilitates the examination of negative affects and the ubiquitous control theme. Typical agreements include weight parameters, meal structure, and accompanying medical examinations.

The therapeutic framework imparts stability and security

A regular meal structure of three main meals and three snacks should be aimed for as a central treatment goal. Due to the lengthy preexisting and self-imposed restrictive eating behavior, patients with anorexia nervosa find it difficult at the beginning of treatment to consume a normal portion of food. Main meals can therefore be divided into several smaller meals. Given favorable cooperation, a high-calorie drink supplement can be temporarily adopted until the digestive system can better process normal meal portions. All information and recommendations pertaining to nutrition (and in particular to portion size) are described in the *Nutrition Guidelines for Patients With Anorexia Nervosa*, see Appendix.

The physical state of patients with anorexia nervosa usually requires medical monitoring of their condition. Consultation with their general practitioner should be undertaken every 2 months, together with general lab work. Depending on specific risk factors such as pronounced purging with laxatives or diuretics, some patients may require more frequent consultations. The assessment of medical risk should follow current clinical recommendations (Treasure, Claudino, & Zucker, 2010).

At the beginning of therapy, it should be made clear to patients that doctors and therapists cannot hinder the possibility of their cheating on or disregarding treatment agreements. However, a responsible handling of the jointly developed treatment agreements should be aspired to. This includes guarding against an unreasonable idealization of therapy by patients that can be accompanied by feelings of helplessness. Patients usually experience relief when idealization is questioned, since they no longer need to fear the "power of the therapist."

4.2.1   Managing Weight

Weight is a helpful barometer in therapy

In the treatment of anorexia nervosa, body weight and its progression are helpful and valuable barometers in the therapy. Until treatment, intrapsychological and interpersonal conflicts were processed within the symptoms of the eating disorder – for example, through starving or purging behavior. A prerequisite for processing underlying fears, affects, and conflicts is therefore the abstinence from symptom behavior. Furthermore, the weight loss and extreme low weight cause an emotional numbness (Brockmeyer et al., 2012). For the price of emotional security, patients take into account that they will also experience positive emotions less intensely. Thus, weight gain is indispensable for the activation of the conflicting relationship patterns, emotions, and wishes around which the therapy is focused.

Central treatment goals are normalization of eating behavior and body weight

Central treatment goals are the normalization of eating behavior and body weight. The following statement applies: "The normalization of eating behavior is not everything, but without it everything is naught" (Schors & Huber, 2003, p. 61). In an ongoing treatment, patients should be monitored once per week prior to the beginning of each session. The weekly goal for weight gain is established as about 400–600 g (not to exceed 1,000 g) (i.e., 14–21 ounces, not exceeding 35 ounces per week). The documentation of weight progression takes place on a weight curve and is recorded by the patient (see the Appendix). At the beginning of treatment, weight should be discussed at the opening of every therapy session until a significant weight gain goal (e.g., an increase of ≥ 1 BMI unit) is reached. The overall weight goal should be set at BMI of 18.5 kg/m², which conforms to the recommendation of the World Health Organization. Furthermore, it is explained that inpatient treatment will be necessary if the patient falls below a set value of a BMI of 15 kg/m² for more than 2 weeks. This a priori agreement simplifies the handling of negative weight developments during treatment.

Particularly during the beginning phase of therapy, the topic of body weight and eating behavior is generally shrouded in an atmosphere of secrecy and "conscious deception" (Bruch, 1978). It is recommended that the therapist openly discusses the possibility of cheating, in the context of the therapeutic agreements and avoids an overly hasty termination of therapy. The cheating behavior exhibited by patients has the function of expressing autonomy and independence or of avoiding humiliation: sometimes phrased by the patient as "while eating I can decide, only I matter in that moment" or "while eating and purging I was my own master, I didn't have to make any compromises."

A frequent occurrence during therapy are pseudo statements of motivation in relation to gaining weight, hiding weight loss by wearing expansive clothing, or manipulating weight while on the scales. For example, the weighing-in allows for extensive manipulation by drinking large amounts of liquids, failing to empty the bladder, or by hiding weights in clothing. For this reason, in the assessment of nutrition status, parameters other than body weight should also be taken into consideration – for example, muscle status, skin condition, and cardiovascular and lab results (Treasure et al., 2010).

Patients often argue that they must first reach a total psychological stability in order to gain weight. This can be interpreted as an avoidance of confrontation with the painful emotions of helplessness and is best treated in a sympathetic yet firm manner. Without a gain in weight, therapy will remain unsuccessful.

Often patients with eating disorders have previous experience with therapy during which they quite possibly gained an understanding of psychodynamic background information pertaining to their illness. This knowledge not only assists recovery, but it can also strengthen defense mechanisms and be used to "blind" the therapist. This too supports the decisive role that weight status and progression represents as a barometer of the therapeutic process.

4.3   General Principles of Therapy

4.3.1   Basic Characteristics of Psychodynamic Therapy

A general principle of therapy is broaching conflicting relationship themes

The psychodynamic procedure focuses not only on anorexia-specific aspects, but it also focuses on conflicts in relationship patterns and the structure-based limitations of emotion processing that cause disruptions in relationships. In Box 5, typical psychodynamic interventions are specified (please compare with Summers & Barber, 2012).

Box 5
General psychodynamic principles of intervention

- A respectful, empathic, accepting, and impartial (i.e., not oriented to personal interests) therapeutic stance
- Facilitation of the patient's freedom of expression
- Empathy with the inner experience of affect and fears and their verbalization
- The broaching of "unacceptable" feelings
- Centering in on interpersonal relationships, especially on repeatedly unfavorable relationship patterns (see Section 3.3.1: Relationship Patterns)
- Connecting current experience to past experience
- Illustration of symptom-triggering situations
- Development of an alternative understanding of conflict situations
- Observation of habitual defense mechanisms and finding an appropriate discourse for them (e.g., by challenging the avoidance of difficult topics during therapy)
- Explanation of the medical complications and consequences of anorexia nervosa
- If indicated, careful determination of unconscious or preconscious wishes, impulses, or anxieties (e.g., by working with dream content)
- If indicated, the handling of tensions in the client–therapist relationship (e.g., wishes and fears in relation to the therapist)

4.3.2   Handling of Transference and Countertransference Dynamics

The relationship with the therapist thrives from the tension between free development and individuality (at times this can present as opposition to, or rebellion against, the therapy) and the rules and boundaries inherent to treatment (that the therapist vigilantly maintains). From a therapeutic perspective, this interaction is best described as a tightrope walk which demands a high level of flexibility by the therapist if a balance between the patient's needy wishes and strivings for autonomy is to be maintained.

Balancing allowing for autonomy and assuming care involves a tightrope walk

The relationship patterns described in Section 3.3.1 clarify the difficulties that must be overcome during the beginning phase of therapy. The therapeutic setting may also promote feelings of helplessness as well as impulses of withdrawal and self-control. These anorexic behaviors can elicit countertransference reactions in the therapist.

From a psychodynamic perspective, how the therapist handles the patient's withdrawal and defenses (which ultimately can elicit feelings of helplessness in the therapist) is pivotal to whether or not treatment succeeds. These feelings must be endured again and again without applying too much pressure or counterpressure on the patient. The ongoing processing and balancing of understanding, with clear adherence to boundaries, allows the patient to learn basic interpersonal skills. The severity and contradictions of anorexia nervosa must continually be kept in mind, and if necessary, the benchmark of therapy success adjusted; even small successes should be recognized and duly valued. This can merely be a feeling of improved atmosphere during a session or a reduction in the therapist's anger when in contact with the patient. Sometimes a time interval and the context of supervision are helpful in identifying these minimal developmental steps.

Typical dangers for acting out a countertransference include the heightened effort to be helpful, which the patient could interpret as a signal of the therapist's own neediness. This can unsettle the patient and heighten defense mechanisms; at the same time, it may strengthen power struggles.

4.3.3   Work on Body Image

A distinctive feature of anorexia nervosa is problems with body image. It is crucial to discuss and process the patient's body image and their fantasies pertaining to bodily functions (Bruch, 1962). The ingestion of food and the gastrointestinal passage through the body are experienced intensely by patients and accompanied by fears of becoming overweight or feelings of disgust concerning eating and digestion. Occasionally, a "primitive" confusion persists regarding the various aspects of digestion and sexual fantasies. To better understand the patient's worries, it can be a helpful exercise for the therapist to focus on their own reactions to ingestion and to help the patient visualize the path that food takes through the body.

Eating reminds the patient that they have a body. Work on body awareness is an essential prerequisite for the subsequent work on self-confidence. By experiencing the body, a basic experience of one's relationship to oneself is made possible. Body-oriented psychotherapy with body awareness techniques, or with imagination techniques that include the body, are viable building blocks in the outpatient treatment of anorexia nervosa. The perception of facial expressions, body gestures, breathing, and perception of the body should be integrated into the therapeutic process. Furthermore, gaining access to physical awareness with specific techniques can help uncover the influence that posture has on both self-confidence and self-awareness, which in turn can increase emotional awareness. For increasing self-awareness, creative imagination techniques that focus on the perception of bodily dimensions as they relate to mood and eating are also valuable therapeutic interventions. Moreover, these techniques allow the patient to experience "hands on" how emotional factors influence the perception of their body. In the ANTOP study, body image dissatisfaction was closely related to symptoms of depression and anxiety; baseline body image disturbance predicted affective comorbidity at the 12-month follow-up (Junne et al., 2016). Body image problems usually increase during treatment. Since body image problems are associated with weight gain and show a high degree of persistence, they should, generally speaking, be an important therapeutic target in the treatment of anorexia nervosa (Junne et al., 2016).

It is important that the patient be guided toward developing a more empathic and friendly relationship to their body. This includes the ongoing lessening of self-damaging behavior such as restrictive food intake, intense sports that put excessive strain on the body, and misuse of laxatives and diuretics. The constant anorexic attempts to control body image by weighing and body checking should be discussed and reduced, step by step.

Awareness of the body should be incorporated in therapy

Patients with anorexia nervosa present with a distorted perception of their body. Current understanding of the disorder does not assume a primary deficit in body perception, but rather a disturbed affective modulation of body perception. This disturbed affect modulation results in extreme discontent with one's body. This perception of the body is closely related to the patient's self-concept. Discontent with one's own body should be changed in such a way that weight and figure no longer exclusively define the concept of body image. In this context, symbolic interpretations lend themselves to handling the distorted body image perception. As such, body perception can be a first step in gaining an understanding of repressed emotions and conflict themes. Examples of interventions are given below.

Intervention Examples
Discontent with body image

Therapist: What does your body want to communicate to you?

Therapist: What would be the message your body would send if it could voice an opinion?

4.3.4 Inclusion of the Family

The following section discusses the possibility of including the primary family in the therapeutic process, especially when treating younger patients. It in no way attempts to describe the interventions of family therapy in their entirety (a more detailed and helpful source of family therapy interventions can be found in Fishman, 2004; Lock & Le Grange, 2012; Selvini-Palazzoli, 1996).

In the treatment of anorexia nervosa, the inclusion of the family in the individual's therapy setting is of great importance. A family orientation session was included in the ANTOP study because it serves to uncover current relationship conflicts. The therapeutic procedure will be briefly described here.

In the family orientation session, diagnostic aspects are in the foreground. During the session, the current relationship conflicts with various family members can be uncovered and used in the therapeutic process. This is especially valuable when stable object representations are missing, which is often the case among a very structurally impaired group of patients. One danger for the therapeutic process is that when conflicts in relationship dynamics are continually trivialized, a counterproductive harmony is manifested.

The orientation session for family members serves to uncover current relationship conflicts

When the patient is directly confronted with their family members in the family session, information can be gathered about intrafamily relationship patterns that could possibly be perpetuating the illness; this session also enables the therapist to observe how the patient enacts their relationship with the family.

For the family session, all members of the primary family (parents as well as siblings) are invited. It is the patient's task to invite them. The goal is to motivate all members of the core family, although it is not an absolute must that all members are present to carry out the family session.

In the event that it is not possible to conduct a family session with members of the primary family, and if the patient is in a relationship or is married, the alternative is to conduct a couple session with the partner or spouse and, if appropriate, also with their children. The contraindication for conducting a family session is any potential for escalated conflict within the family, which can be linked, for example, to family violence.

Example for the Organization of a Family Session

Enough time should be allotted for greetings and a getting acquainted phase. Ideally, the therapist has a short exchange with each family member to establish personal contact with friendly small talk. Before the main topic and conversation guidelines are shared, each family member should have the opportunity to talk to the therapist ("How did the family get to the session today?"; "What profession or role does each family member have?"; "Who lives with whom, and where?") It is important that the therapist establish a connection with each member of the family – this is sometimes referred to as the joining phase.

The central topic of the preliminary phase of the session is relief from any imagined blame. For many parents, siblings, and partners, a family session is often synonymous with clarifying the question, who is to blame for the illness?

When opening the family session, the technique of circular questioning can be helpful

The topic of illness can be approached in various ways. One possibility is to ask each family member which topic they would like to see discussed during the session. This can occur through the use of *circular questioning* (e.g., the patient may be asked, "What do you think your father believes is an important topic?"). Alternatively, each family member can be asked for their subjective understanding or belief about how the illness has manifested itself.

To mitigate the parents' feelings of being blamed, the multifactorial origin of anorexia nervosa and the lack of scientific proof for a prototypical anorexic family can be discussed. The involvement of family is instead most important for the course of anorexia nervosa; each family member can help the patient overcome the illness. While exploring the family system, or while trying to uncover dysfunctional patterns of family interactions, additional themes of interest could be the characteristics of the illness as understood by family members, any perceived threats to their relationships and future plans within the family, effects of the illness on family life and on individual family members, and accessible resources.

During the session, family members are given an opportunity to ask questions about the illness. It is recommended that general information be given pertaining to the potentially life-threatening aspects of the illness, the danger of chronicity, and the consequences of starvation. Finally, recognition of the emotionally challenging support that parents and/or partners have given in an attempt to deal with the illness should be recognized and appreciated. An emphasis can be placed on resources within the family, and their self-efficacy should be strengthened. Especially when working with younger patients, the therapeutic alliance with parents and their engagement is crucial to treatment success.

During preparation for a family session, many patients express doubt about the reasons for, and benefits of, such an encounter. Several ways of addressing these doubts are as follows:

Intervention Examples
Addressing misgivings before the family session

Therapist: Maybe you are worried about what could be uncovered and which emotions could bubble up, including your own, when everyone gets together here?

Therapist: What are you expecting? How will your parents react when you reveal how you are really feeling?

Therapist: Our experience is that problems and anxieties are often left undiscussed in families. The family session can be a venue in which such topics can be discussed.

In spite of (or perhaps because of) the frequent doubts that surround the family session, the results of the family sessions are often very positive.

The following examples describe possible reactions of the patients:

Intervention Examples
Patient's reactions

Patient:	The family session was also important. At first my father didn't want to participate, but it was really important to me that he did. During the family session, I noticed for the first time that my relationship to my father makes me extremely sad. Previously, I had always accepted our bad relationship without a word of protest.
Patient:	While growing up I never learned to confront conflicts, and I was never really honest. During the family session, this became clear, and I felt like I was sitting next to strangers. A lot of things weren't talked about in our family. I have learned to be honest with myself and also with others. I can now accept my weaknesses more easily and express my feelings to others.

Family Work in the Absence of the Family

If neither a family session nor a couple session can take place, we suggest speaking with the patient about the effect that their illness has had on their family system, in the absence of the family.

The approach of circular questioning can also be used effectively when family members are not available. This type of questioning can be used to better understand the connection between the patient's symptoms and their meaningful family relationship themes (e.g., "What do you think your mother suspects is the cause of your illness?"; "What would your mother say about this?"; etc.). This circular questioning technique can also uncover resources and capabilities that can prove to be important for the patient's recovery.

As an alternative or an extension to circular questioning, techniques taken from Gestalt psychology can be used. Gathering information on the meaning and impact the illness has had on the family system can be used during therapy (Agras et al., 2004; Lock & Le Grange, 2012; Selvini-Palazzoli, 1996), the same as with a family session. Therapists who have practical experience with alternative techniques and methods of communication can draw on these for support – for example, using a family board or genogram.

4.4   Treatment Setup and the Initial Phase

The entire treatment program consists of 40–50 sessions and can be divided into three phases with the key themes described in the

following section. This subcategorization is a suggested orientation guideline only. Individual therapies may require adjustments
regarding time spent on each therapy phase, and it may also be necessary to include additional content. Therefore, this setup depicts
a model from which individual therapies may vary significantly.
Furthermore, the contents of each phase are only suggestions that
can help structure the therapy and set priorities in the phases; the
content included is not limited to these phases.

4.4.1　Diagnosis, Therapeutic Alliance, and Deriving the Focus

At the beginning of therapy, the psychodynamic interview serves
to define the therapy foci, as is prescribed by the OPD-2 (see also
Chapter 3). When working with patients with anorexia nervosa,
the initial phase of psychotherapy is often accompanied by a lack
of insight regarding the state of their illness, and a pronounced
ambivalence toward treatment. Due to this psychological mind set,
therapists must embrace an empathic, supportive, but also active
therapeutic stance. It is recommended that at the onset of therapy,
the therapeutic framework be discussed with the patient (*pact talk*),
and depending on the patient, more or less information should be
provided regarding the disorder and course of treatment.

The psychodynamic interview serves to define the therapy foci

During this initial phase, therapeutic goals are determined, especially regarding the goal of weight gain (see Section 4.2.1: Managing
Weight). However, together with weight gain, other important
themes and therapy goals are processed. These themes refer to the
patient's subjective goals and are gathered from classical themes in
therapy, such as overcoming maladaptive relationship patterns.

4.4.2　Basic Therapeutic Stance

Due to the pronounced ambivalence that patients have to treatment
and the central importance that weight gain plays in the success
of therapy, therapists must adopt and maintain a directive and
prescriptive approach to their interventions. The therapist should,
especially in the initial phase, actively strive to convince patients
that treatment is required. In this approach, the risks and consequences of anorexia nervosa should be discussed and explained.
Experience shows, however, that mere appeals to the patient's
health consciousness are generally not successful in gaining their

motivation for treatment. Appreciative and empathic interventions are therefore particularly important.

Intervention Examples
Supportive aspects

Therapist:　It really is a shame that your illness kept you from going to college.

Therapist:　I believe that you don't deserve to be as lonely as your anorexia is making you.

Not uncommonly, patients express their ambivalence by prolonged silence; this necessitates active interventions. In this context, for example, the therapist's perceptions can be shared with the patient. Reflections concerning the problems that arise during treatment onset can also be communicated at intervals.

Intervention Examples
Patient's prolonged silence

Therapist:　Are you having difficulty in finding a way to talk about your feelings?

Therapist:　What needs to happen so that you can trust me (or the therapy)?

Therapist:　Are you hoping that others will see your distress and not just continue to criticize you?

Additionally, an agreement should be made with the patient that during the first 4 weeks of treatment (or a maximum of 6 weeks), body weight should remain stable without losing or gaining weight. In our experience, it is of critical importance to the therapeutic alliance to not create additional pressure by suggesting weight gain during the initial phase – otherwise, the therapist can be trapped in the role of being just another "persecutor." Furthermore, the first 4 weeks should be used to systematically prepare for weight gain; the therapist can, for example, consider the following questions: How is the patient going to inform her social environment? Who can she turn to, when she needs help or support in changing her life once therapy begins and change proves difficult? How can she create optimal conditions to handle upcoming challenges?

During therapeutic interaction with the patients, it should be implicitly clear that they are more than just an anorexic person. It is advantageous if the patients can feel that a *pact* against anorexia nervosa is emerging. The therapist can then become an ally, not a "persecutor."

> **Clinical Pearl**
> **Basic therapeutic stance in the initial phase**
>
> Creating a secure framework, giving structure, focusing in on anorexic behavior while explicitly avoiding pressure, empathizing with the natural fears of the patient, verbalizing inner experiences, coping with personal helplessness.

4.4.3   Working on the Therapeutic Alliance

It is important during the initial phase of therapy that possible obstacles to success are addressed (e.g., fear of gaining weight, fear of becoming too dependent, fear of helplessness, being at the mercy of therapy). It can be helpful to anticipate how life could be in 5 years' time after the anorexic disorder has been resolved.

Patients value the therapist's expressions of empathy regarding the demanding and paradoxical nature of anorexia nervosa. Due to the constant inner "terrors" of this severe illness, patients often feel a yearning for support. The anorexic modus operandi has often become the inner voice of the patient that is followed obediently and without question. The destructiveness of this anorexic life design, coupled with emotional impairment, can result not only in emaciation but also in social isolation; this is often denied by patients.

The therapist's empathic exploration of the anorexic world facilitates a stable relationship

Thus, developing an inner awareness of the dysfunctional role that anorexic behavior has is an important prerequisite for treatment motivation. The identification of proanorexic beliefs and thoughts is described in detail in Section 4.4.4 (Uncovering Proanorexic Beliefs).

During the initial phase of therapy, interventions that demarcate the immense power the anorexic voice has over the patient should be implemented. As a next step, the therapist can encourage the patient to verbalize any mental experiences and perceptions they have that contradict the anorexic modus. If the patient remains overly ambivalent and progress in treatment is lacking, the therapist should address this issue early on. Working with pictures or metaphors can be helpful in this case.

> **Intervention Examples**
> **The "inner advisor" anorexia nervosa**
>
> *Therapist:* What thoughts go through your mind when you are considering eating or not eating something?

Therapist: Do you have an inner advisor that forbids you to eat food? What happens when you ignore this inner advisor?

Therapist: How can we succeed in silencing your inner anorexic advisor and build trust in the therapy?

Therapist: What is necessary for you to trust me as much as you trust your inner anorexic voice?

For therapy purposes, the symbolic expressive character of the anorexic disorder should be used

Another possibility is using phrasing that metaphorically transforms relationship patterns into a food context. This technique can help to gradually link the eating (or not eating) primary experience with a relationship context. The overall goal is to establish in the patient a curiosity regarding their perceptions, thoughts, and feelings.

Intervention Examples
The symbolic character of anorexia nervosa

Therapist: How could you regain your appetite for life?

Therapist: What message do you think not eating food and not swallowing gives?

Therapist: You are conveying a message with your weight – namely, a worry that you are not being seen or respected.

Therapist: Is all the pressure you are putting on yourself making you smaller and giving you the feeling of literally disappearing?

Therapist: Does the constant weight loss also express an inner exhaustion of resources, as if you were trying to say "I just can't anymore"?

The greatest benefit and strength of the anorexic modus operandi is that the anorexic disorder is a loyal companion and never leaves the patient alone. Diluting or relinquishing this pattern is connected with intense affect and a great loss for the patient. Because the mechanisms that maintain the pattern exist on all levels – psychological, interpersonal (with parents, siblings, teachers, and friends), and biological (hunger metabolism) – it is necessary to achieve improvements on all three levels to effect recovery.

Ambivalence is not a state worth lingering in

The patient's ambivalence can be viewed as a natural part of the transformation process. It is obvious, however, that the prolonged coexistence of conflicting feelings and thoughts creates increasing stress. Management of the patient's inner conflict activates emotions and fears that can be used in the transformation process. The goal should be to strengthen those personality traits that motivate a weight gain. This calls for a high level of flexibility on the part of the therapist. In the course of each intervention an attempt should be made to avoid entangling argumentation (i.e., to pursue "dancing not wrestling"). In addition, an empathic attitude on the part of the therapist and an acceptance of the frequent back-and-forth in the course of the treatment process allow for the right amount of openness and support. This enables the patient to develop new perspectives on the illness and new ways of handling it.

Intervention Examples
Ambivalence

Therapist:	It could be that apart from the fear of gaining weight, there is another aspect that is hindering you? Maybe it's that you currently show others by your physical state that you need help and affection, which you otherwise have difficulty showing or expressing directly.
Therapist:	Admitting that something is wrong with your weight and your body would imply frightening consequences; others might then ask what is wrong with you and would tell you what to do.

Observations from the ANTOP study corroborate the idea that illness insight is sometimes missing entirely. The phobic avoidance of emotions as well as the pacification of food-related problems during the initial phase complicate response to treatment (Clinical Vignette 4).

Clinical Vignette 4
Avoidance of affects and denial of illness

Therapist:	What thoughts or feelings go through your mind when you think about beginning treatment? Do doubts or fears crop up?
Patient:	No, I'm happy to finally start treatment and I hope that the therapy will be successful.
Therapist:	How are things going right now with eating? How do you feel while preparing your meals or eating your food?
Patient:	Yes, it's going well. I prepare my meals in the kitchen, and then I take them with me to the balcony. With this wonderful weather we're having, it's really a treat to eat outside.
Therapist:	Does eating represent indulgence and pleasure to you?
Patient:	Yes, it's always been that way for me.
Therapist:	Is there maybe another side to eating within you? A side of eating that has a different connotation? What

Patient: does that side feel like for you, when you are preparing a meal or getting ready to eat the food prepared?

Patient: I prepare my food in such a way that I like eating it. The only thing is, I always have to leave a little bit leftover. I just can't seem to eat the entire portion. I don't know why that is, I can't really explain it.

For patients, the participation in therapy ultimately means learning to live with fears of an uncertain future as well as sadness for the time of their life they have lost due to the disorder. For this reason, it is crucial in the initial phase of treatment to look at the advantages and disadvantages of the changes that will occur in the patient's future, and to accentuate the fact that there is always freedom of choice.

4.4.4   Uncovering Proanorexic Beliefs

A good therapeutic approach to the illness involves a discussion of the often covert *proanorexic beliefs and thoughts* (i.e., which positive roles does the anorexic disorder fulfill for the patient?). According to Serpell, Treasure, Teasdale, and Sullivan (1999), the most common positive reinforcers of anorexia nervosa are emotional security, a sense of control, feelings of attractiveness and self-worth, and the avoidance of negative emotions (see Figure 3). The illness allows for emotional security as well as an overall feeling of being someone special. The anorexic disorder also helps regulate emotional closeness and aloofness. The fact that it reduces emotionality and emotional vibrancy is seen by the patients as having positive as well as negative aspects.

> Anorexia nervosa patients experience their symptoms as ego-syntonic

The goal of learning for the patient to accept the less prominent and critical voice of anorexia nervosa can be supported using the "Letter to Anorexia Nervosa as a Friend" (see Box 6). Therapeutic writing can initiate a self-reflection process that can be used in subsequent steps of treatment. Furthermore, this intervention is a valuable instrument for registering the level of motivation a patient is experiencing at the time. Some typical topics that arise in the patients' own versions of the letter, such as a "Letter to Anorexia Nervosa as an Enemy," are feelings of being at the mercy of the illness; anger and fury at the illness; social withdrawal, together with the loss of friendships and relationships; abandonment of education, employment, and career goals; feelings of having wasted time; not taking part in life; current physical ailments and fear of

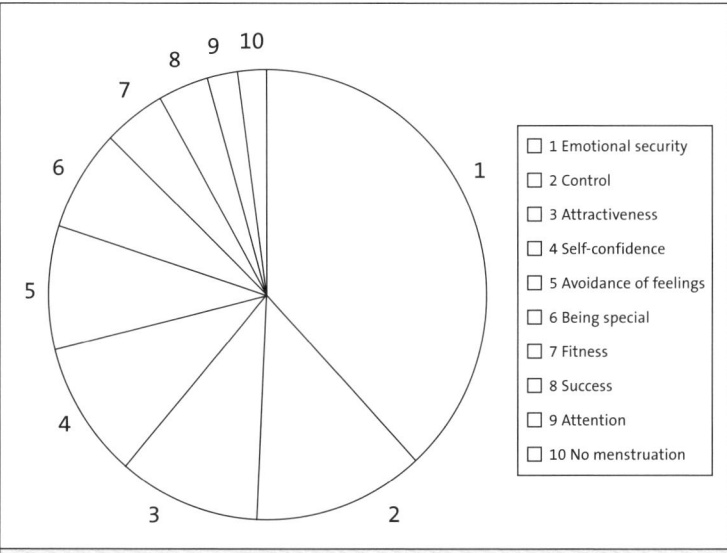

Figure 3
Proanorexic beliefs. The size of the sections in the above graph represents the frequency with which each of the ten proanorexic beliefs have been reported in a population of patients with anorexia nervosa. Adapted from Serpell et al. (1999, p. 182).

future medical problems; depression and irritability; feelings of having been tricked by the illness.

An advantage of this intervention is that the patient has the opportunity to autonomously identify deep-rooted attitudes, behaviors, and relationship patterns in the course of the writing process.

Analysis processes focusing on aspects of illness should be actively initiated

Box 6
Example of a letter to anorexia nervosa as a friend

Dear Anorexia,

You were always there for me when others ran out on me or abandoned me. You are a loyal companion and have often helped me. Others think that you are injuring me, but the truth is that your support helped me survive. Without you, I would have been aimless and lost, like a satellite in space. You give me something that I can concentrate on when my world threatens to fall apart, and you give me back a bit of the control that I have lost.

4.4.5   Focusing in on Self-Esteem Problems and Depressive Experiences

Focus on the self-worth theme Patients with low self-esteem show a higher treatment dropout rate and a poorer treatment outcome (Halmi et al., 2005; Wild et al., 2016). Due to these findings, it is important to integrate interventions that strengthen the often fragile self-esteem experienced in the initial phase of therapy. It is important to regularly use statements of appreciation and expressions of understanding regarding the patient's high standards.

The initial goal should be the identification and transformation of negative beliefs about the self, as they have an obvious influence on self-esteem. Negative beliefs often determine the basis from which experience and behavior (i.e., ego-syntonic) is initiated. A crucial first step, therefore, is to question these dysfunctional beliefs in order to turn them to being ego-dystonic. One technique involves contrasting emotional experiences with a rational interpretation of negative beliefs. Another possibility is supporting the patient to take an outside perspective when differentiating between feelings and the reason-driven interpretations of negative beliefs. Identifying exceptional situations, in which the patient feels both competent and self-confident is an additional technique.

Intervention Examples
Handling negative beliefs

Therapist: If you could slip into someone else's shoes and look at yourself from an outsider's point of view, would you still come to the conclusion that you are unlikeable? How would your friends and relatives judge you?

Therapist: You say that you felt small and helpless in this situation. In retrospect, what is your assessment of the situation now? Can you see differences between your feelings then and your rational evaluation right now?

Therapist: When was the last time that you really felt strong and resilient when relating to other people?

Aside from their negative self-concept, patients may also show a dominant overly adapted behavior or superficial conformity (other than in relation to their eating behavior) and act in an exceptionally well-behaved manner out of fear of criticism. At the same time, they may have a negative appraisal of others. They are often perceived as being forceful, dominant, and controlling (cf. Section 2.1.2: The Interpersonal Dynamic). Such feedback from their social environment is also destabilizing to their self-esteem.

Intervention Example
Overassimilation

Therapist:	The people who are always nice and well behaved aren't necessarily always appreciated. They notice that other people are using them, but they're afraid of peoples' reactions if they were to say no – as if everything would then be lost.

Furthermore, anorexic patients often regulate self-esteem by intense pursuit of achievement and a high level of perfectionism. A careful questioning of the patient's intense pursuit of achievement and perfectionism should be attempted, but in a circumspect manner.

The patient's overly "well-behaved" behavior and intense pursuit of perfectionism should be questioned

Intervention Examples
Perfectionist expectations of self

Patient:	I'm only loved when I'm really perfect. I only have value when I don't make any mistakes.
Therapist:	It's hard to watch how much pressure you put on yourself. It's like you're trying to be superhuman.
Therapist:	What would you lose if you were less self-critical and less achievement-oriented?

After patients have begun taking part in treatment, most suffer from intense episodes of depression; the established interventions developed for depression disorders then become applicable (Leichsenring & Schauenburg, 2014). Interventions that address disruptive black-and-white thinking, self-punishing tendencies, and overly harsh self-criticism (*superego pathology*) should be applied.

Clinical Pearl
Avoiding power struggles

In the initial phase of treatment, the greatest danger for the therapist is getting locked into a power struggle about eating behavior and weight. If this occurs, the patient will inevitably feel helpless and inferior and begin a process of inner devaluation.

4.4.6   Amendments to the Initial Phase

Toward the conclusion of the initial phase of therapy, the family session described in Section 4.3.4 (Inclusion of the Family) can be conducted. Our experience shows that it is preferable that the family session not take place too early in treatment, because it is best that patients are given the opportunity to reflect on the meaning and contradictions of their disorder before communicating with their family members.

A separate aspect of treatment during the initial phase is the sociotherapeutic support of school, the workplace, etc. In this context, it is vital to support the patient in learning to ask for help on various levels. Furthermore, patients should receive information on healthy, routine, and balanced nutrition, as described in the guidelines provided in the Appendix.

Clinical Pearl
Overview of important interventions in the initial phase

Supportive Interventions:

- Constructing a beneficial therapeutic relationship (empathy, support, acceptance of affect experience in a nonjudgmental manner)
- Attempting to identify with their split-off submerged aspect of life
- Reinforcing self-esteem (acknowledging, relieving their conscience, modifying demands on the self)
- Supporting situations in which the patient feels like the initiator of competent actions
- Both patient and therapist should be aware of the possibility of remission and discuss change (Caution: The therapist must guard against countertransference of helplessness).

Structuring Interventions:

- Informing the patient about the risks and consequences of anorexia nervosa
- Discussion of proanorexic patterns and beliefs
- Motivation – "Letter to Anorexia Nervosa as a Friend" (or Enemy; Section 4.4.4)
- Analysis of the interrelationship between eating behavior, interactional relationship dynamics, and associated affects

---

4.5   Middle Phase (Working With the Focus)

The middle phase of therapy should address the previously identified relationship dynamics and structural foci. The prerequisite for this therapeutic work is the establishment of a viable and stable therapeutic alliance.

4.5.1 Basic Therapeutic Stance

In the middle phase of therapy, structuring and guiding interventions should be reduced, to encourage a working alliance between patient and therapist. Weight goals must still be continually monitored. Ideally, the following characteristic psychodynamic interventions are implemented:

- identifying and understanding problematic experiences, including problematic experiences in the therapeutic relationship (focusing on affective components);
- supporting an exploratory trial-and-error approach to the main difficulties.

Responsibility for control of weight goals should increasingly be transferred to the patient

---

Clinical Pearl
Therapeutic stance in the middle phase

In this phase a somewhat less directive approach and the avoidance of a controlling and educational attitude are employed. If applicable, a reduction in control of weight goals, together with an increase in the handling of affect contents should be implemented.

4.5.2 Focusing on Affective–Emotional Experiences

After a few weeks, the weight gain process begins to support the patient's ability to perceive their own emotions. These emotions are often interpreted as being forbidden, and they may take on an overall threatening character (i.e., anorexia nervosa is used as an "anesthetic"). The handling of the constant preoccupation with food, body, and eating has become predictable and controllable. In comparison, feelings are neither predictable nor controllable. The patient may be surprised by how angry or furious they can feel. At first the patient's anger is directed toward topics of eating, weight, or figure, regardless of the fact that the actual addressee of their anger is the therapist whose help they would rather not have. Upon relinquishing their typical controlled demeanor, the patient becomes confronted with the fear of experiencing their own jealousy, vindictiveness, greed, etc. At this crossroads in the therapeutic process, it can be helpful to examine how the patient experienced themselves before therapy began.

In the middle phase, interventions should be used that intensify the affective-emotional experience

To enable the experience of emotions in an enlivened and perceptible manner, several interventions can be implemented within the current therapeutic relationship (Clinical Vignettes 5 and 6; cf. McCullough, 2003).

> **Clinical Pearl**
> **Interventions that support the affective–emotional experience**
>
> - Mirroring and clarifying affects
> - Offering relief from affect ("permission")
> - Intensifying affect experience ("delving into")
> - Establishing a connection between affects and relationship experiences
> - Identifying the triggers of affects
> - Assigning affects to the present and the past
> - Developing distance from affects

Patients should learn to perceive how affect experience is linked to eating behavior

Clinical Vignette 5
Insight into the connection between affective–emotional situations and eating behavior

Therapist: It seems difficult for you to address problems that stand between yourself and your parents.

Patient: Yeah, um, exactly – there are many situations where I don't dare show my parents the anger that I'm feeling when I talk with them.

Therapist: What is your worry? What could possibly happen if you talked about your anger?

Patient: I don't know, I've never thought about that before. Maybe because I just don't trust myself and then jump to an overly hasty conclusion about what might hurt my parents. I often feel too heart-broken and angry to talk about that with my parents.

Therapist: It seems like you are worried that you might hurt your parents?

Patient: Yes, partly I am. I'm worried that I won't be objective in such an emotionally strained situation, and so I tell myself that it's better not to talk about it at all.

Therapist: What influence do these situations have on your eating behavior?

Patient: On those days I really have trouble eating anything at all. I think I punish myself for my intense emotions by not allowing myself to eat.

Therapist: Let me see if I've got this straight: You are taking the anger that you feel toward your parents and directing it onto yourself by not allowing yourself nourishment and by ultimately accepting the consequences that weight loss has on your body?

Patient: Mhm, yes, in principle that sounds right.

Therapist: Your parents seem to have a lot of characteristics that you appreciate, but some of their traits bother you. It's normal that you sometimes disagree. How could you show your parents that you are angry? It's important to be able to show personal boundaries.

Patient: Mhm, yes, in some respects I don't want to be like my parents.

Therapist: Yes, that is an important and central question: What kind of a person do I want to be? Your eating behavior seems to be an important alarm signal in the sense that it lets you know when you are not expressing your own ideas or feelings in the relationship with your parents.

Clinical Vignette 6
Intensifying the affective–emotional experience

Therapist: You seem very aware of what you eat in comparison with what your boyfriend eats.

Patient: Yes, I do notice that, that's true. When he eats more than I do, I'm relieved, and I don't have the feeling that I've eaten too much. However, when I eat more than he does, I immediately feel uneasy and have the feeling that I ate way too much.

Therapist: How do you experience those situations when your boyfriend eats a small portion? Is your experience such that you really don't feel hungry anymore, or do you forbid yourself from eating more even if you're still hungry?

Patient: My throat tightens up, and I feel sad or angry, and I no longer feel like eating. I don't feel hunger in these situations.

Therapist: How can it be understood that you react so intensely in those situations? What are you afraid of?

Patient: I don't know – maybe that I might gain weight, that I won't be able to stop eating.

Therapist: So it's about control? Let's suppose that you would eat more than your boyfriend, what feeling would come up?

Patient: A fear, a fear of being too greedy – a glutton, a person that doesn't have herself under control.

Therapist: And then ... what are you afraid of?

Patient: I don't know.

Therapist: Where do you have that feeling in your body?

Patient: In my throat and in my legs, like a shakiness in my legs.

Therapist: Stay with that shakiness in your legs. What other feeling could be there?

The issue of unacceptable affects should be broached

Patient: The fear of being weak and helpless, the fear of being a failure.

Therapist: You're afraid that if you show your fear you might become weak and helpless?

4.5.3   Additional Work on the Relationship Focus

The psychodynamic approach to psychological illness is based on the idea that certain dysfunctional relationship experiences in early childhood constitute lifelong vulnerability factors that then interact with genetic predispositions as well as additional life experiences, and eventually culminate in disorders. Consequently, like other psychological illnesses, anorexia nervosa is preceded by the perception of internal or external dangers within relationships. These dangers initiate the unfolding of maladaptive relationship patterns, as discussed in detail in Section 3.3.1 (Relationship Patterns).

Maladaptive relationship patterns represent important material for therapeutic work

The formulation of the relationship dynamic focus should aim to clarify the relevant relationship themes as defined by the focus (Box 7 and Clinical Vignette 7). All other problem areas that are not subsumed under the focus should receive less attention. The interventions are closely affected by the typical relationship themes seen in anorexia (see Section 3.3.1: Relationship Patterns). (Please note: The therapist could attempt to communicate the focus of maladaptive relationship patterns to the patient so that them themselves can check its validity in everyday life.)

Box 7
Interventions for work on the relationship focus

- Differentiating the subjective relationship experiences ("What exactly do you mean by ..."; "I haven't fully understood what it was that you experienced when ...")
- Distinguishing between perception of self and the perception of others ("In this situation you felt as if ...; I wonder how X felt?")
- Determining active and reactive aspects of personal behavior ("Did you act out of fear, or because you wanted to attain X?")
- Uncovering in part ambivalent paradoxes in the construction of personal relationships (i.e., anorexia nervosa as a dysfunctional pattern of the wish for more attention and parental devotion, fear of closeness in spite of the wish for relationship, excessively subordinate behavior in social comparison processes)
- Working out the cyclic maladaptive pattern in relationships (self-fulfilling prophecy) and the dysfunctional effects on self-perception
- Working on hidden wishes and fears (in an advanced stage of therapy)

- Working on the relationship patterns within the patient–therapist relationship when applicable (i.e., interpreting transference: "Could it be that it is hard for you to talk about X here, because you are afraid that I wouldn't take you seriously?")
- Developing therapy goals and perspectives based on the relationship focus (i.e., changes in relationship patterns with others: "What could you suggest as a viable goal with regard to these unfortunate recurrences?")

Clinical Vignette 7
Work on the relationship focus

Conflicting relationships should be discussed

Therapist:	What is it about your mother that makes you so mad?
Patient:	I'm angry because in my mother's eyes, I always do everything wrong: I'm not raising my children right; my house isn't tidy enough; you have to be ashamed of me because I'm so skinny.
Therapist:	Mhm (affirmative). So I have the feeling that you are always being criticized, no matter what topic you introduce with your mother.
Patient:	She isn't as critical with my sister. Even if we do something the same way, it's not seen as the same for my mother.
Therapist:	You have the feeling your sister and you are being treated differently. How do you express your anger and unhappiness to your mother?
Patient:	At times I am able to express my anger in some situations. Just yesterday I told her that it is none of her business how we go about doing things.
Therapist:	How does your mother react when you say something like that?
Patient:	Then she gets angry. She said, "You can't keep going on like this."
Therapist:	How is it for you when you vent your anger like that?
Patient:	On the one hand, I think that I might have been a bit direct and mean-spirited. I think she is ashamed of my illness, but on the other hand, that is none of her business anymore. It's my life. She shouldn't meddle in my life.
Therapist:	So, do you feel relieved, or do you have a guilty conscience?
Patient:	Afterwards I do have a guilty conscience. I have the impulse to go by her place and drink a coffee with her. By now I've gotten used to the fact that nothing is how it used to be. I haven't been over at her place in a while, and I'm okay with that. And yet I would like to go for a

visit – it doesn't have to be every day. But I know that even if I try it again, it's not going to work out.

Therapist: How would you wish it to be?

Patient: That she learns to accept me and my life, the choices that I have made, that she acknowledges the way I am trying to raise my kids and that she doesn't criticize me nonstop.

Therapist: And have you ever said that to her?

Patient: No, not really.

Therapist: Why not?

Patient: Yes, well in those situations she gets just furious.

Therapist: Mhm, so you're worried that saying something would cause even more quarreling?

Patient: I really would – I would really rather move away. But that's easier said than done.

Therapist: Mhm, that would mean moving away from your parents in order to create a physical distance.

Patient: Yes (wearily), but that probably wouldn't change anything either.

Therapist: Why do you give your mother so much power over you?

Patient: Mhm, I've never asked myself that.

Therapist: In my opinion, a part of you really likes your mother. What would it be like if all of a sudden your mother would approach you and praise you – praise you for managing your life even with your illness, and ask if there was any way she could help?

Patient: (Becomes sad and begins to cry.) I always wished that exactly that would happen.

4.5.4   Level of Structural Integration

A low level of structural integration means that basic psychological coping mechanisms are not at the patient's disposal (see Chapter 3 of the OPD-2; OPD Task Force, 2008). With anorexia nervosa patients, it is often an open question whether these impairments are due to situations of extensive childhood deprivation, situationally as the result of chronic starvation, or due to extensive chronic inner conflict or delayed development such as that caused by the anorexic disorder itself. Regardless of the cause, it is often prudent to assume that patients are not able to do certain things due to the impairments of their disorder and not – as is often the case in conflict situations – because they subconsciously do not wish to do certain things. This calls for an empathic and supportive approach

A low level of structural integration requires a less confrontational approach

during extended periods of therapy rather than a confrontational approach. Several possible interventions that address structural difficulties (as described in Section 3.3.3: Structural Impairments) are depicted in Clinical Vignette 8.

Clinical Vignette 8
The case of Ms. I.

Ms. I. is in her mid-40s with haggard facial features; she is living with restrictive anorexia nervosa that she has had since her youth. At her orientation visit to the outpatient clinic, she presents with a BMI of 16 kg/m². The recommendation for further care came from the clinic that had previously treated her after she was admitted with extreme low weight (BMI at clinical admission: 11 kg/m²). Her current weight is the most she has weighed since the illness began when she was 13 years old. Even though she has usually had a critically low weight of BMI 15 kg/m², she was, with medical help, able to give birth to three children.

Contact with the patient is difficult; she controls the conversation and remains pale and inanimate; she regularly ends the session on her own accord 5 minutes before time is up. Due to her excessive control, any flexible handling of wishes or affects is obviously very constricted. Aggressive impulses are countered with self-deprivation or bound up in "masochistic" appearing excessive exercise. She feels totally overburdened and under extreme pressure from her three children, and by her profession and her housework. In addition, her husband is often away on business. She is unable to care for herself or accept the help she needs.

Specific therapy sessions that took place in the case described in Clinical Vignette 8 are presented in the following sections (Clinical Vignettes 9, 10, 11, 12, & 13), along with the interventions that were applied to address structural deficits in the areas of affect experience and differentiation, impulse regulation, self-worth regulation, acceptance of help, and detachment.

Clinical Vignette 9
The case of Ms. I.: Affect experience and affect differentiation

Therapist: The weight curve shows multiple episodes over the past 3 months where you temporarily lost 2–3 kg (4.5–6.5 lb). Can you remember what was different in those phases?

Patient: Mhm, no, I don't know.

Therapist: Could it be that those episodes coincided with the business trips that your husband took overseas?

Patient:	Let me think. Yes, that pretty much fits with the dates of his trips.
Therapist:	I feel overwhelmed when I think about you having to organize all of that alone while your husband was overseas.
Patient:	That really doesn't make a difference, since my husband always works really late and just comes home to sleep.
Therapist:	Mhm, regarding your eating behavior it does seem to make a difference. I think it could be important to look at what that difference might be.
Patient:	I can't really see any connections.
Therapist:	I have the feeling that you often stop eating and do lots of exercise, when you feel lonely and stressed.
Patient:	(Wearily) I haven't noticed that yet.
Therapist:	Maybe it's important for you to be independent and self-reliant to manage everything on your own without outside help? I can remember another patient that was in a similar situation. At the end of treatment, she reported feeling relieved not always having to be "the strong one," and always having to do everything on her own. For years she had denied needing others. Her relationships gained intimacy; she thought that was something really nice. I think you also have an inner voice that is wishing for support and closeness to others.

This case vignette illustrates the patient's lack of consciousness of personal needs and stress. It is an example of frequently observed affect avoidance and the limited affect differentiation often seen in patients.

Adressing affect phobia is challenging

Helpful interventions for encouraging the experience of affects and their differentiation include mirroring emotions, making affects available by sharing the therapist's experience or using examples of others, and giving a detailed analysis of the associations between situational conditions and eating behavior. The following excerpts illustrate additional examples of these interventions.

Overcontrolling self-regulation should be questioned tactfully

Clinical Vignette 10
The case of Ms. I.: Impulse regulation

Therapist:	Right now you are totally focused on the children and not aware of your own wishes or needs. Will you be celebrating your birthday this year?
Patient:	Yes, well. I looked at the calendar already and noticed that the date is right in the middle of the week. But I

Therapist: don't want to invite anyone ahead of time, whoever thinks of me can come by the house for a piece of cake.

Therapist: How would you feel if a good friend of yours forgot your birthday and didn't stop by or call on your birthday?

Patient: Yes, I would prefer not finding out who hasn't called, or not even be at home to accept calls. I wouldn't be mad at her, but I would immediately think: "Oh my, did she forget me?" It is nice if one is remembered on their birthday. Well, that has always been somewhat ambivalent for me.

Therapist: It sounds like you are experiencing two needs that are in conflict with one another. On the one hand, you would like to celebrate your birthday and to invite friends over, and on the other hand you are maybe worried that you might get disappointed and hurt.

Patient: Do you celebrate your birthday?

Therapist: Now you are changing the conversation. It seems you are having difficulty talking about this conflict with me?

Patient: Yes, maybe.

Therapist: Let's first address the need that you are more familiar with – Agreed?

Patient: Okay.

Therapist: What are you closer to right now, celebrating your birthday or not celebrating?

Patient: Not celebrating my birthday.

Therapist: Okay, let's take a closer look at this need. Try to answer this for yourself, why would you prefer to not celebrate.

The patient in Clinical Vignette 10 is showing difficulty in fulfilling her own wish for celebrating her birthday with friends. Generally, anorexic patients show the tendency to be overly controlling; drive wishes and affect are thereby countered with a defensive behavior of increased self-control. This influences and limits the patient's interactions and opportunity to communicate with others. The aim of the intervention is to facilitate the recognition of intents to act in person and possibly uncover inner contradictions, and to promote the development of the patient's ability to achieve inner compromise.

Negative
introjects should
be identified and
handled

Clinical Vignette 11
The case of Ms. I.: Self-Worth regulation

Patient: Now I remember: "unfit to live life." That was what my mother said. I would be unfit to live my life. And in certain respects, she's right.

Therapist: That is a harsh opinion coming from your mother's mouth. If you heard this insulting sentence today – that you are unfit for life – how would you answer today?

Patient: Being unfit for life could also mean having two left hands; I don't think that is so bad.

Therapist: Hm, your mother was pretty direct and extreme in her opinion.

Patient: Yes, my mother can be very strict and critical.

Therapist: Do you have that same voice in you? The voice that is hard and unrelenting towards others?

Patient: (Pause) Yes, I think so, yes.

Therapist: Can you think of an example?

Patient: I'll have to think about it. Well, there is this secretary at work. I sometimes lose my patience with her. She always acts so helpless, you have to explain everything 100 times, and then it's still better if you do it yourself. How can it be that she has gotten this far in life? Actually, in my eyes, she doesn't deserve it. She is like a dead weight. The rest of us drag her along. She isn't even able to organize enough paper and envelopes for a job. If I were the boss, I would kick her out. I wouldn't have any qualms about it. That may sound harsh, but she is being paid to do nothing; the rest of us are dragging her along, and she does nothing. I don't have any empathy for moochers. You know those people that use others.

Therapist: And are you as strict with yourself as you are with others?

Patients should
learn to replace
negative beliefs
of oneself and
others by more
realistic thoughts

The patient exhibits a negative mother introjection due to early experiences of invalidation and rejection by her mother. She exhibits a negative self-concept with a fragile self-worth experience. The behavior of others is interpreted as being either overpowering and domineering, or inadequate and incompetent. The therapeutic contact should be used specifically for the internalization of a supportive and positive object. This leads to an increase in positive feelings toward the self, to a decrease of overly critical feelings toward others, and a decrease of self-criticism. Furthermore, negative introjections should be examined and excessive black-and-white thinking questioned. A further intervention goal should involve promoting a tolerance for feelings of shame and uncertainty.

Clinical Vignette 12
The Case of Ms. I.: Accepting help

Therapist: There are people that can accept help, and others that have a problem accepting help. To which group do you think you belong?

Patient: I always thought that I was engaging with others and accepting help from them. But my colleagues offered their opinion, that I am totally withdrawn and that they know very little about me. That really surprised me because I had judged myself in a different light.

Therapist: Is your behavior different when you interact with your husband, friends, colleagues?

Patient: Well, we are how we are. I probably act to the same towards my husband, my colleagues, and my parents, but it's also clear that one has different topics for different people. You know how it is, when you know that a person only likes hearing one thing or the other, or when you know that he really likes talking about cars, then you talk about that with him more readily.

Therapist: Do you entrust others with your interests, problems, and ideas?

Patient: I am interested in other people. Sure, when someone says, tell me about yourself, how was your vacation. Then I would tell them something about myself and say my vacation was nice or so.

Therapist: So you don't miss disclosing who you really are in conversations?

Patient: Well, you know if I get a phone call, I really like that. I like that a person is interested in me and I think: "I have to give that back," so that the person calling isn't hurt and thinking that she's never ever calling that conceited cow again, who doesn't even ask how I'm feeling.

Therapist: I'm getting the picture that you avoid closeness in relationships again and again, out of fear that you might lose your real self.

Throughout the therapy sessions in Clinical Vignettes 8, 9, 10, 11, & 12, the patient has described her relationships and contact situations with her husband, friends, and colleagues in a very monotonous and normative manner. In relationship situations, she is mostly interested in her counterpart; she refrains from confiding her own personal views or problems. Through this neurotic compromise, she avoids experiencing the feelings of closeness and connectedness that she sees as threatening. A basic consequence of

The patient should be empowered to allow closeness

being unable to express attachment is being unable to accept support and caring from others. During treatment, possibilities should be explored that allow for emotional connectedness to others. The therapeutic relationship as well as social situations outside of the treatment setting that allow for in vivo exposure can be used to this end. An important antifear function is to generate anticipation for the reactions that others could have.

Clinical Vignette 13
The case of Ms. I.: Detachment

Following the cancer diagnoses of Ms. I.'s mother, a crisis situation of extreme weight loss ensues. The patient's weight loss plunges below a BMI of 14 kg/m², necessitating a period of temporary clinical treatment. After 2 weeks of inpatient treatment, Ms. I.'s physical stability is such that she can resume outpatient treatment.

On a superficial level, the patient seems not to need others. Nevertheless, an existential dependency exists for supportive objects like her mother. The anticipated fear of losing her mother is so extreme that she is no longer able to regulate this fear with positive inner objects or respond adequately to the help offered her. She reacts with a relapse of anorexic symptoms. The crisis represents an important phase in therapy in which the inhibiting affect of fear is replaced with the experience of sadness and anger. This contributes to an improvement in the patient's affect competence and affect regulation.

Generally, the treatment of anorexia nervosa includes working through impending developmental stages while at the same time, addressing and restructuring fear. During this process, a balance between exposure to affects and resource orientation should be the aim. The described interventions can be applied to patients who have a moderately integrated structure level. Patients of the binge-eating/purging type can, at times, show a low level of structural integration, as found in an emotionally unstable personality structure. The structure level can be obscured by the consequences of being extremely underweight and the associated leveling of affect. When treating these patients, practitioners should include interventions that address the specifics of severely structurally disordered patients. In this regard, we would point to the extensive literature on the elements of psychodynamic treatment regarding the therapy of personality disorders (see Clarkin, Fonagy, & Gabbard, 2010).

4.6 Closure Phase

The limitations that arise in the course of implementing a time-based psychodynamic focal therapy are often overestimated. Our experience with this misconception proved itself during the ANTOP study. Over the course of the study, the duration and number of therapy sessions at 40 sessions was adequate for over one third of patients. It is important to accept the reality of this limitation from the beginning and to consider it in the planning phase of therapy (we refer to this as *seeing therapy from the closure point*).

4.6.1 Basic Therapeutic Stance

By the end of therapy, the therapeutic relationship and the therapeutic work alliance are an important relationship experience for patients suffering from anorexia nervosa. Within the framework of a positive therapeutic relationship, many patients have, for the first time, given up socially distancing themselves from all relationships and have increased trust in themselves, with their needs and wishes. The end of the therapy thus inevitably activates fears of separation and loss. Sometimes, but by no means every time, this is accompanied by a resumed increase in anorexic impulses. Central relationship conflict themes such as separation fears that often manifest and had already been processed during the middle phase of therapy, resurface in this new context. If the painful feelings of abandonment, anger over separation, and disappointment are allowed, they can be used to support the development of independence. Against this background, at least 12 sessions should be reserved for the closure phase.

In the closure phase, separation fears and feelings of abandonment get reactivated

Consequently, the last phase of therapy is concerned with the promotion of autonomy and personal responsibility, along with the continued handling of the central relationship themes. Inevitably, patients experience doubts toward the end of therapy about whether or not they will be able to maintain their new behaviors in the absence of therapeutic support. The therapist's implicit message should be one of confidence in the patient. Furthermore, the therapist should specifically mention the patient's successes and positive development during therapy to support their sense of achievement and to raise positive expectations for the future.

Intervention Examples
Ending the treatment

Therapist: Are you experiencing this as though the end of therapy automatically implies a relapse to your old helplessness?

Therapist: What was your experience, and how did you feel when therapy didn't take place this past year during vacations or holidays?

Clinical Pearl
Therapeutic stance in the closure phase

Promoting autonomy with a willingness to *let go*. Discussion of separation and parting, saying goodbye.

4.6.2   Stabilizing New Skills

The approaching end of therapy confronts both the therapist and patient with concluding questions such as, To what extent were the initially drafted therapy goals reached, and what was reached overall? The overall goal during the closure phase should be the stabilization and consolidation of achievements. Therapists should reinforce the patient's self-confidence in the newly developed structures. Even small achievements should be duly recognized. In this vein, the perspective of a supervisor, who has observed the therapy at intervals and with less personal involvement, can be helpful in identifying even small successes. In retrospect, the pivotal moments and experiences the patient had during therapy should be addressed, and their role in shaping new experiences described. It is also recommended that amendments to past coping strategies and conflict patterns are recognized by the therapist as steps toward maturity and a new orientation. A point should be made to attribute the achievement of specific goals and subgoals to the patient in order to strengthen self-efficacy. Finally, addressing those goals that were not attained and formulating concrete steps for the months following treatment are important steps in the closure phase.

The initially drafted therapy goals should be balanced with the patient

---

Intervention Example
Appreciation of accomplishments

Therapist: If I compare your reaction today with how the situation was a year ago, I notice that ...

4.6.3   Applying New Skills in Day-to-Day Life

The greater intervals between sessions toward the end of treatment can be used to try out autonomous developmental steps. Upcoming tasks and current real-life problems are brought into the spotlight. In anticipation of the conclusion of treatment, the focus should be on the concrete implementation and testing of newly acquired skills, as well as on handling related problems. The patient learns to integrate the experiences gained with the therapist into their day-to-day life, without the support of the therapeutic setting. Self-management techniques are deliberately encouraged. Both occupational and personal arrangements subsequent to treatment should be planned and discussed.

The therapist should strengthen the patient's self-reliance

4.6.4   Anticipating Relapses

In addition to everything else in the closure phase, possible relapses should be anticipated and discussed. Recommendations regarding how to approach these topics include the following:
- identify critical situations;
- summarize helpful strategies.

Together with the patient, situations can be recalled in which relapses occurred in their past. By looking at these situations, a model (functional schema) can be drafted that describes the patient's personal and transpersonal experiences that led to the relapse. The analysis of relapse situations illustrates that often there is a time frame leading up to the relapse, in which alterations in mood and behavior are discernible. The patient's awareness should be sensitized to these early signs of relapse.

The handling of relapses should be proactively discussed

Based on the patient's past experience, helpful strategies for handling relapses are discussed. Coping strategies can be evaluated based on their usefulness and whether there are additional self-damaging aspects of relapses to be considered. In the event that it is concluded that previous attempts have failed, therapists can actively help patients look for and try new coping mechanisms.

Because in a great number of cases, anorexia nervosa is a lengthy and tedious illness – although by no means in all cases (Zipfel, Löwe, Reas, Deter, & Herzog, 2000) – it is important to convey that relapses most often occur in the course of difficult life tasks. The sense of responsibility that patients must develop entails returning to healthy strategies and behaviors as soon as possible after a relapse. If the situation is still unstable directly before treatment termination, it may be expedient to identify people within the patient's social network who can be contacted in case of a relapse to the anorexic modus (this does not necessarily entail a loss in weight). An additional safety net can be a weight boundary that is communicated to the general practitioner; when the patient falls below this boundary, renewed therapeutic consultations can be agreed upon.

4.6.5   Persistence of Symptoms

The disappointment of unattained goals should be handled

The therapeutic management so far described for the closure phase of treatment has assumed a generally or partially successful therapy. In the event that weight development remains stagnant, or an inability to independently regulate healthy nutrition persists, the conclusion of therapy requires a different approach.

The therapist should assume the role of *helpful companion* expressing solidarity with, and support of, the patient. The careful structuring of the further organizational process – in anticipation of the completion of therapy – has the function of minimizing fear and avoiding feelings of helplessness. The necessity of further outpatient, day clinic, or inpatient care is discussed with the patient. Possible support structures within the patient's social network are identified, including consultant and supportive institutions. This resource-oriented approach also includes identifying and appreciating the patient's inner resources.

Affects concerning self-doubt, resignation, or aggressive impulses directed at the therapist should not be analyzed during this therapy phase. Instead a modified therapeutic stance should be adopted. The therapist should, figuratively speaking, stand at the patient's side and adopt the role of mentor (or coach) and together with the patient examine and attend to any feelings, thoughts, and impulses related to the end of therapy.

4.6.6   Follow-Up Care

Anorexia nervosa is a psychosomatic illness with a high risk of chronicity. Despite intensive therapeutic efforts many patients continue to show a persisting symptomatology (weight phobia, restricted eating, excessive endurance sports, purging behavior, bulimic attacks, etc.). After therapy ends, we recommend a therapy break of at least 3 months for those patients who are physically stable, regardless of whether or not they show a complete persistence of symptoms. The break allows patients to practice new behavior and implement new skills in their day-to-day lives; it gives them an opportunity to gather experiences using the skills learned in therapy and to see its influence on their life. Also, feelings associated with loss and farewell are avoided in a seamless continuation of therapy. Frequently, the greatest and most significant changes in behavior occur after the completion of treatment, as patients can then begin to act autonomously, in full awareness of their responsibility for themselves. It is advisable that general practitioners monitor their anorexic patients for at least 1 year posttreatment (to check lab tests, weight, eating behavior, and psychosocial health). With this approach, relapses can be identified early on, and continuation of treatment initiated if necessary. During the first year after outpatient therapy, booster sessions spaced at large intervals can not only allow the reactivation of therapy themes but also facilitate processing of problems and challenges. In the event that a patient exhibits an exacerbation of anorexic symptoms and a drastic loss in weight during the closure phase, additional treatment is warranted. This is also true if the increase in symptoms and weight loss occurs just after the end of treatment.

Even after successful therapy, anorexic patients should be monitored for 1 year posttreatment

The following chart (Box 8) is a summary of the various stages of therapy and the central themes of each phase.

Box 8
Summary of the therapy phases and themes

Initial Phase (up to approximately the 15th session):
- Psychodynamic interview following OPD-2, deriving a focus
- Explaining setting and structure of therapy content
- Determining the therapeutic framework
- Defining therapeutic goals
- Handing out nutrition guidelines
- Establishing a therapeutic relationship
- Working on motivation and insight into illness
- Discussing the ego-syntonic quality of anorexic behavior
- Focusing on self-worth, self-acceptance
- Activating resources and a supportive working style
- Delineating the connection between eating behavior, relationship dynamics, and associated affects
- Including family: orientation session with family or partner

Middle Phase (up to approximately the 30th or 40th session):
- Determining the therapeutic approach (more structure-focused, more conflict-focused, or mixed focus on structure and conflict)
- Focusing on guided problem activation
- Working on the relationship focus

- Focusing on affective–emotional experience
- Intervening to stabilize structural weaknesses

Closure Phase (starting at about the 30th or 40th session and continuing until about the 40th or 50th session):
- Actively broaching the end of therapy
- Balancing out therapy and stabilizing achievements
- Implementing and experimenting with new behavior
- Discussing goals not achieved
- Developing concrete developmental goals for after therapy
- Preventing and handling relapses
- Planning occupational and personal courses of action for after therapy
- Suggesting aftercare and, if applicable, follow-up treatment

4.7   Procedural Challenges

Crises and problems during treatment of anorexia nervosa are more often the rule than the exception

Crises and problems in the course of treating anorexia nervosa are more often the rule than the exception. The emergence of unavoidable and sudden crises should therefore be considered. The following subsections present guidelines and helpful strategies.

Weight gain leads to the reactivation of emotions in all their intensity. During this stage, the occasional risk of reactively expressing those activated emotions emerges (e.g., self-injuring behavior, excessive endurance sports, etc.). Initially, experiencing affects is coupled with the feeling of total loss of control, which is then resisted and suppressed (i.e., not feeling anything is the perfect state of being). Furthermore, weight gain expresses an acting-out of indulgence and a forfeiture of self-determination. Allowing for the satisfaction of personal needs, such as nourishment and feelings of security, sexuality, and care, is equivalent to forfeiting the anorexic identity, coupled with a threatening to ego functions.

4.7.1   Strong Ambivalence

Possible interventions: Contrasting the persisting and the progressive components of the patient's personality (this can lead to the patient's increased self-acceptance of even the more rebellious aspects of their personality).

4.7.2 Setting a Weight Goal (When Patients Are Unable to Formulate One)

Possible interventions: Working with various personality parts: "What weight goal would that part of you have that doesn't want to gain weight?"; clarifying distressing affects: "What is your apprehension, what do you think could happen, if you set a weight goal for yourself?"; exploring fear of commitment and surrender; and defining the fundamental freedom of choice.

4.7.3 When Patients Hold Onto Their Anorexic Behavior, Even When Negative Consequences Escalate

Possible interventions: Attempting to find a playful rather than an adversarial approach; encouraging the patient to develop possible solutions instead of the therapist's providing them.

4.7.4 Weight Loss in Therapy, Particularly in Regard to Weight Manipulation

Possible interventions: Drawing a boundary, while simultaneously showing understanding for the fear-inducing effect of weight gain; discussing avoidance as it pertains to therapy (as the only topic being discussed in this case is weight); discussing one's "guilty conscience" toward oneself and the therapist. (Note: A weight of BMI < 14 kg/m² indicates the need for urgent inpatient treatment.)

4.7.5 Newly Emerging Bulimic Behavior

Possible interventions: Identify trigger situations, interactions, affects; strengthen impulse control by developing alternative strategies; avoid acting out countertransference (i.e., disappointment, anger); identify newly activated fears; use metaphors and pictures that establish a connection to the relationship dynamic focus.

4.7.6   Self-Injuring Behavior

Possible interventions: Along with the process of identifying trigger situations, it is recommended that the therapist take an empathic but clear stance with regard to this behavior. The therapist should stress that self-injuring behavior is incompatible with the therapeutic setting (i.e., taking over and strengthening the patient's self-care). Important symptom-oriented actions are contracts that the therapist implements in cooperation with the patient (e.g., a pact against self-injuring behavior).

4.7.7   Medical Complications, Such as Dehydration

Possible interventions: Close cooperation with a colleague experienced in the medical complications of starvation is required so that any untoward developments can be addressed in a timely manner.

4.7.8   Meddling by Others – For Example, Family

Possible interventions: If the patient is not able to establish boundaries between themselves and their primary family and unable to reflect their role as the carrier and mediator of unreal performance requirements and ideals, then *indirect* work with the family can be tried.

4.7.9   Handling the Indication for Inpatient Admission

At treatment onset, the lower boundary weight of outpatient treatment should be defined

Possible interventions: From treatment onset, it is important that boundaries are set for both weight and medical symptoms that require urgent inpatient admission. These strict boundaries should consistently be acted upon without necessitating a break in the therapeutic relationship.

4.7.10   Excessive Endurance Sports

Participating in excessive sports in an almost compulsive way can hinder therapy goals with regard to weight gain; it is best to address this early on in therapy. Furthermore, physical complications that arise due to excessive sport, in combination with reduced bone density, should be taken into account (Herzog, Minne, et al., 1993; Zipfel et al., 2001).

Possible interventions: Here too, symptom-oriented measures in the form of a contract between the patient and therapist can be implemented. Physical activity should be reduced to a level that is compatible with the current weight and daily calorie intake, while sports that strengthen muscles and guard against osteoporosis can be recommended. Classical endurance sports such as jogging should be avoided.

4.8   Adjuvant Therapies

4.8.1   Adjuvant Therapy With Psychopharmacology

The eating disorder guidelines of the American Psychiatric Association and of NICE (APA, 2006; NICE, 2017) argue that previous randomized controlled trials (RCTs) could not prove a significant benefit when psychotropic drugs were used in addition to psychotherapy. Accordingly, there are no psychotropic drugs approved for the specific therapy goal of weight gain for the treatment of anorexia nervosa. Treatment of a psychiatric comorbidity can be carried out according to the guidelines for the particular disorder. However, in this context it is important to mention that symptoms of depression and obsessive-compulsion disorders respond well to weight gain. Also, selective serotonin reuptake inhibitors (SSRIs) appear to be of limited antidepressive efficacy during extreme low weight and limited tryptophan intake.

To date, there is no evidence for the efficacy of psychotropic drugs on weight gain

Nevertheless, in some cases, it can be important to administer medication during the treatment process. For instance, when a severe episode of depression presents along with sleep disturbances, the importance of treatment with an antidepressant should be discussed. Furthermore, weight gain can be significantly hindered by a severe case of compulsive behavior that can, potentially, be influenced through the use of an adjuvant psychotropic drug. Another group of symptoms that might benefit from supportive medication are any self-injuring behaviors. Particular attention should be paid to cardiovascular side effects; this is especially relevant for drugs that lengthen the QT time on an electrocardiogram.

4.8.2   Adjuvant Intake of High-Calorie Dietary Supplements

High-calorie dietary supplements can be helpful. Particularly during the re-alimentation phase at the beginning of treatment, the gastrointestinal tract is unprepared for normal amounts of food due to the prolonged period of fasting and underweight. Many patients report an uncomfortable feeling of bloating and pain during digestion. In this phase, a high-calorie dietary supplement can support weight gain goals by providing the necessary calories in the form of snacks. The application of these supplements is best reserved for the re-alimentation phase of therapy. It should be the patient's goal to work on increasing their nutrient ingestion step by step, so that energy supplements can eventually be dispensed with.

5 Case Examples

The following sections cover some case studies for different types of anorexia.

Ms. P., Age 26, With Anorexia Nervosa, Binge-Eating/Purging Type

Ms. P., age 26, presented with anorexia nervosa of the binge-eating/purging type. After a preliminary interview at the psychosomatic clinic for outpatients, she agreed to treatment within the framework of the ANTOP study.

Psychodynamic Interview

A tall, slim woman in elegant and figure-flattering clothing arrives for treatment. At intake, she presents herself as flirtatious, though a pronounced uncertainty is noticeable. At the initial treatment session, the psychological strain this has on her is not immediately discernible. Her weight at the beginning of treatment is 50 kg (110.2 lb); her height is 171 cm (5 ft 7.3 in) (BMI 17.1 kg/m²).

The patient reports that her eating disorder began with restrictive eating behavior when she was 15 years old. Her starting weight then was 58 kg (127.9 lb); initially she lost weight until she weighed only 47.5 kg (104.7 lb). This weight remained constant for many years until last year when she again lost weight to a new all-time low of only 40 kg (88.2 lb) (BMI 13.7 kg/m²). After an initial phase of purely restrictive eating behavior, pronounced bulimic binge-eating/purging symptoms developed at about the 2-year mark. The patient reported multiple binge-eating/purging attacks per day, which occurred not only at her workplace during the day, but also at home when her boyfriend was not present. When asked about a possible trigger for the eating disorder, the patient reported being on the swim team during that stage in her life, but that she felt excluded from the team of her older girlfriends.

Concerning her treatment motivation, Ms. P. reported that her boyfriend was the determining factor for her seeking treatment. With his support, she had managed to gain weight, from 40 kg (88.2 lb) to her current weight of 50 kg (110.2 lb). During the weight gain phase, her boyfriend had monitored her weight daily and motivated her to continue gaining. At 50 kg (110.2 lb), she noticed that an inner barrier had been reached and that she was no longer able to continue overcoming the disorder solely with her boyfriend's help. She reported suffering from her ongoing preoccupation with food, weight, and figure.

Ms. P. reported taking part in her first outpatient treatment for anorexia nervosa when she was 17 years old, at the rate of one or two sessions per week. She prematurely discontinued her treatment after only 5 months, as she did not feel that her symptoms were improving.

Professionally, Ms. P. works in marketing. Pursuant to her college studies, she was offered a position in the company where she had done her training. She still works for the same company. Her relationship status has been stable over the past 6 years, and she has been living with her boyfriend.

Ms. P. reported growing up in her primary family with her older sister. Her maternal grandmother lived in a small apartment in her parent's house and was an important comfort to her. Her grandmother was like a second mother to her. Ms. P. told her everything, and her grandmother was always there for her. The patient moved out of her parents' house 6 years ago and began renting an apartment with her boyfriend. Shortly after she had moved out, her grandmother fell ill and needed nursing care; she passed away 3 years ago.

Ms. P. reported that her mother's pregnancies had been very difficult. Before the birth of the patient's older sister, her mother had suffered two miscarriages. While her mother was pregnant with the patient, a "fractured pelvis" became problematic shortly before her delivery date. (Presumably this is a reference to the loosening of the pelvic ring; background information or a specific time frame were unclear to the patient.) Her birth progressed without complications. Her father had always wanted four girls ("organ pipes"). After her mother's second pregnancy, the patient's birth, a gynecological operation was necessary that hindered further childbearing.

She described her relationship with her mother as problematic. Her mother was often moody, loud, and discontented with herself and others. The patient's mother had always defended the kitchen as her domain. The patient recalled baking cookies with her grandmother because she was afraid of dirtying her mother's kitchen. A very sad memory for the patient was that her mother often secretly threw presents into the trash that Ms. P. had made for her. Her father worked as a high school teacher and was described by her as a loving, heartfelt person. He was conservative in his views and focused primarily on safety and achievement. Nevertheless, she also had nice memories of her childhood. Her parents were very supportive of their children's hobbies and extracurricular activities: "They really went the distance." During childhood, she showed a highly adapted behavior. Conflicts with her parents began to increase with the onset of her eating disorder. For over 2 years, Ms. P. succeeded in keeping her eating disorder and self-induced vomiting a secret. When her parents finally found out that their daughter suffered from a binge-eating/purging disorder, they were disappointed and saw this as a betrayal of trust. The patient's relationship with her sister was one of sibling rivalry; she was more successful and achievement-oriented than her sister. The relationship to her sister began improving when she was about 16 years old and was described as currently good.

Selecting a Focus

Ms. P. grew up with a strict, dominant, and often critical mother. The mother appears to have acted in a socially distanced manner toward her daughters. The maternal grandmother therefore became Ms. P.'s most important psychological parent from whom she experienced security, encouragement, and acceptance. Furthermore, the atmosphere within the family was tainted by competition as well as sibling rivalry with her sister who was 2 years older. The experience of being excluded from her peer group, combined with maturation fears, could potentially have initiated the onset of her eating disorder at age 15. From then on conflicting points of view and self-assertion in her relationship with her mother found their expression in the eating disorder. In reference to central themes of conflict, the patient was most likely suffering from a self-worth conflict and a self-sufficiency versus need for care conflict. In both types of conflicts, the mode of processing was predominantly active.

Relationship experiences with her dominant and aloof mother, as well as rivalry with her sister, shaped the patient's primary pattern of interaction. Both experiences transferred to her peer relationships, resulting in her current social isolation. Apart from her boyfriend, Ms. P. had no friends. She was tied to her boyfriend as the only source of an accepting relationship, but experienced

difficulties in expressing her wishes for encouragement, acceptance, and security. This dynamic was mirrored in the relationship
pattern where the patient used her disorder to get attention from
him. In the structural diagnosis, Ms. P. exhibited a moderate to
high level of structural integration across all axes which is why the
therapist chose a conflict-oriented therapeutic approach.

Beginning Phase of Therapy

Especially helpful for building an interpersonal relationship between
the patient and therapist is the establishment of an agreement for
weight maintenance in the first 4 weeks of therapy. This takes the
pressure off the patient during the initial stages. At treatment onset,
Ms. P. was very focused on body weight and daily variances in
body weight. She felt extremely unsettled because she could not see
the connection between the changes in her weight and food intake.
Furthermore, the patient felt terrorized by her thoughts and feelings
concerning her figure. She complained of a disproportionate distribution of her body shape (e.g., "bony on top and too curvy around
the bottom"), and also about her negative body sensations (e.g.,
"fear, when I feel my thighs rub up against one another"). In this
early phase of therapy, the therapeutic stance was one of providing
a secure framework and structure (i.e., "standing on the side of the
patient") which was experienced as supportive by the patient.

During treatment, a systematic analysis was carried out – together
with the patient – of the thoughts and feelings that preceded her
binge-eating attacks. In addition, psychoeducational interventions
were used to set up a regular meal structure. The recommendations
in the therapy manual regarding centering in on experiences of
self-worth were helpful. In the analysis of her relationship with her
boyfriend, it quickly became clear that Ms. P. behaved in a very submissive manner and adapted to her boyfriend's opinions. This behavior was acknowledged jointly by the patient and therapist, and the
patient was encouraged to increase her willingness for conflict, and to
express her wishes and needs to her boyfriend in a more open manner.
Experiences of self-worth were identified, together with instances of
negative affect, such as a depressive mood or boredom that preceded
(and are potentially the cause of) her binge-eating attacks.

At this time, Ms. P.'s job situation changed. Her department
closed down, and it was unclear whether or not she would be able
to continue her employment with the same company. Surprisingly,
over the course of treatment there was a long interval where Ms. P.

was not aware of the pressures and emotionally stressed work environment that had often led to binge-eating attacks at the workplace. It was in this context that the patient's perfectionism and transfer of her negative emotions to compensatory eating behavior became clear. As Ms. P. was in an application phase for a new job, this was used to focus on her experience of self-worth and her current resources. The patient was increasingly able to differentiate between her affect experiences and to allow herself to have emotional experiences. However, not much changed in her daily binge-eating attacks nor in her fear of weight gain above her "barrier" weight of 50 kg (110.2 lb) – more specifically described as a fear of gaining too much, too fast. According to the manual, in this treatment phase, the structural framework is to be augmented with a recommendation about how often the patient should weigh herself per day, with a weight gain goal of 500 g (1.1 lb) per week. Moreover, intensive work was done to increase Ms. P.'s impulse control and to develop alternative behaviors in stressful situations.

Gradually, the patient developed competencies in identifying the interpersonal idiosyncrasies that influenced her eating behavior. By processing numerous relationship episodes that occurred either at work or with her boyfriend, it became clear that Ms. P. most often behaved in an altruistic and helping manner. It was very difficult for her to disagree or contradict anyone else; she did not feel that she could impose her own needs and wishes on others. The more able she was to present herself as a whole individual with interests and emotions, the more her binge-eating attacks decreased and the better her overall condition became. The patient and therapist jointly uncovered a cyclical behavior pattern in her relationships which motivated Ms. P. to try alternative behaviors in her interpersonal interactions.

Middle Phase of Therapy

When working on the relationship focus in the middle phase of therapy, the description of psychodynamic intervention techniques for the regulation of emotions is pivotal. Examples are techniques that intensify affect experience (such as allowing for emotion, offering relief from affect), and strategies that assist the patient in finding distance from strong emotions.

Ms. P. was increasingly able to express trust in the therapy and accept her sadness by crying openly. It gradually became clear that one of her greatest fears was that her boyfriend might leave her: "If he knew how I really am, he would quit our relationship." In this respect, it was very important for the patient to invite her boyfriend to the family session, but not her parents.

Her partner was extremely burdened emotionally and began the partner session very directly with the sentence: "Had I known what I was getting into, I would not have begun this relationship!" He seemed perplexed and helpless, and at the same time worried about his girlfriend. During the partner session, the focus was on expressing appreciation for the great job he had done supporting his girlfriend in her handling of the disorder. He was seriously involved in supporting her to gain weight from 40 (88.2 lb) to 50 kg (110.2 lb). He acknowledged, however, that caring for his girlfriend and keeping up his own interests was a balancing act. In the course of the therapeutic conversation, intensive work was undertaken regarding the discovery and cultivation of topics of common interest to the couple – topics distinct from the eating disorder. In addition, the pressure of keeping watch over his girlfriend's progress was relieved by the therapist reiterating that Ms. P. was currently under closely structured therapeutic monitoring. Ms. P. responded to the close scrutiny of dependence and independence in her relationship by losing 2 kg (4.4 lb) before her next session.

An additional stressor at this time started with the beginning of Ms. P.'s new job. It quickly became obvious that the same maladaptive relationship constellations were being reenacted at her new workplace. From the outset she placed high demands on herself; she expected to accomplish her work to everyone's satisfaction, even without specific training. Based on worries of not meeting requirements, she avoided asking for help or for any support through job training. Her fears of not meeting new requirements caused an increase in binge-eating attacks at the workplace. It was possible to work with Ms. P. intensively to enable her to assert herself in new situations, develop a strategy to handle mistakes, and find a way to ask the "troublesome" colleague for help. These success experiences reduced the frequency of binge-eating attacks and supported the weight gain goals; Ms. P. was now able to continuously gain 200 g (0.4 lb) per week. Her weight gain coincided with an increase in dissatisfaction with her body; this was discussed in detail. According to the recommendations of the manual, the discrepancy between selective perception of self and perception of others was used to analyze her dissatisfaction with her own body. The patient felt supported by the encouraging feedback given by her boyfriend, her parents, and colleagues. Despite her weight gain, Ms. P. managed to abstain completely from further episodes of self-induced vomiting.

Closing Phase of Therapy

In the course of the patient's recovery, new problems about her relationship with her boyfriend were uncovered. Ms. P. began to occupy herself with wedding plans and the prospect of starting a family. Because of this, her boyfriend experienced extreme pressure; at the same time he became uncertain about his feelings for her. Both the indecisive quality of their relationship and the imminent end of therapy activated detachment fears. The additional therapeutic process was therefore focused on developing self-assertion and autonomy. Toward the end of therapy, Ms. P. succeeded in handling conflicts in relationships and in broaching difficult emotional topics. The timely preparation for the conclusion of therapy allowed time for the patient's fears and doubts. She expressed her fear about her ability to maintain the goals she had reached – which was discussed over the course of multiple sessions. This resulted in strengthening Ms. P.'s self-efficacy. It was possible to conclude the treatment after 40 sessions. It became clear that the patient had benefitted from therapy. By the end of treatment, her weight was 57 kg (125.7 lb) (BMI 19.5 kg/m²).

Ms. R., Age 19, Anorexia Nervosa, Restrictive Type

Ms. R., age 19, a university student and cellist in a renowned orchestra, arrived at the outpatient psychosomatic clinic with anorexia nervosa of the restrictive type. She voiced a goal of receiving treatment by participating in the ANTOP study. The study had been recommended to her by a colleague in private practice.

Psychodynamic Interview

A well-groomed, stylishly clothed younger looking patient arrived for the psychodynamic interview. She spoke fluidly and eloquently. Her soft facial features were a notable contrast to her emaciated body. Initially she presented herself as seeking help, while at the same time remaining detached and scrutinizing; she was worried that she would be seen as incapable of participating in therapy and sent away. From an emotional perspective her sadness and fear of the future were most noticeable.

At the beginning of treatment, her weight was 45.8 kg (101.0 lb) with a height of 167 cm (5 ft 5.8 in) (BMI 16.4 kg/m²). Her current weight had been stable for the past 6 months. She had reached her maximum adult weight 14 months ago at 55 kg (121.3 lb), her lowest weight occurring just 7 months before at 44 kg (97 lb). The weight loss was arrived at by restrictive eating behavior in the form of very small meal sizes without indulging in prohibited foods, while at the same time participating in moderate sports activity. Due to her extreme low weight, she had refrained from participating in sports over the last few months. Her thoughts were constantly preoccupied with food – which bothered her but did not interfere with her school performance. She would have liked to gain weight and saw her reflection as skinny at times, but not so at other times. She became conscious of her eating disorder because of an argument with her best friend who had acted, she said, "in a confrontational manner" because of her continual weight loss. She also had accused her of being cold and hard. Because of this argument, their friendship broke up. Ms. R. felt deceived and misunderstood; she had only wanted to spare her friend from the troublesome details regarding her problems with weight. She could not identify a trigger for her eating disorder, and could not pinpoint the starting point. Over the past year she had suffered from amenorrhea – an issue that greatly disturbed her and which was, she thought, a "sign of illness". Furthermore, she was afraid of not being able to have a family in future. She also suffered from a general joylessness that had slightly improved since moving out of her parents' house 3 months ago. Initially (shortly before she moved away from home) an outpatient therapy had failed because the therapist thought she had a lack of insight into the illness and was, therefore, untreatable.

Ms. R. grew up in a small town where she lived in a household with her biological parents and younger brother who was 5 years younger. Both parents had an academic degree and had met during their studies abroad. Her father (age 50), after a series of remarkable promotions, worked as executive manager for a well-known company. Her mother (age 52), who had emigrated from Spain, had also been professionally successful before the birth of her second child (the patient's brother). After his birth, she had assumed the role of a housewife. Ms. R. was therefore raised bilingual, between two cultures, she said. During her grade school years, she had been harassed because of her Spanish roots ("Spaniards stink"). Her southern upbringing was oriented around traditional strict values such as respect and politeness, but was, at the same time, indulgent and heartfelt. Her father had always been on a "60s trip" and believed that children, first and foremost, needed freedom in their development. Achievement was important to both of her parents; however, they were not of the same opinion on most other parenting topics. This often caused tension, stress, and frustration in the family, especially for her mother who often blamed the father. Her mother had always wished for a happy family life and was very happy while the children were young. Her father, on the other hand, had achieved everything in his professional life and now wanted to have fun and "stay forever young." As both children gradually became independent, her mother had had to reorient herself. Two years ago, she began a second degree in Spain and often flew there to complete coursework. Because of her advanced age, she was having difficulty finding an internship near her hometown. As for Ms. R.'s brother, after considerable scholastic problems he went to a boarding school for a few years. His indolent behavior had pushed both parents to their limit. Apparently, he had been "analyzed" many times and amply supported with extracurricular tutors. She described her brother as a "jovial and unhurried type," as well as sensitive and expressive, and that they felt close to one another.

From an early age, the patient assumed the role of the link (or mediator) between her parents; she felt strongly about maintaining solidarity within her family. She felt especially close to her mother and felt a similar emotionality and innocence, which left Ms. R. vulnerable. At the same time, she felt she had a single-mindedness and perseverance reminiscent of her father. Ms. R. was very ambitious and committed. She was the valedictorian at her music school, played the cello in a renowned orchestra, worked with dedication on several committees, and enjoyed playing squash and running cross-country.

With regard to physical development and age-specific interests during puberty, the patient reported that she had been "very slow." In Grade 11, when she was on a 3-month exchange program to France, she experienced her first intimate contact with a young man her own age. She would have enjoyed a longer stay in France, but her parents called her back to Germany for financial reasons. The real reason was that her mother, who relied on their close relationship, was feeling lonely because of the separation. Her father, however, had not noticed this, as he was always away on business trips. Just 9 months ago, after a 1-year relationship, the patient had separated from her first steady boyfriend because she felt like she "just couldn't fight on all fronts anymore." Her high school graduation – plus the chaos at home – had put a lot of demands on her, resulting in her boyfriend feeling like a stopgap. She had grieved for the separation for a long time afterwards. His thoughtfulness had made her feel good, and as a result she had become less dependent on her parents. Although her circle of friends had "separated to all corners of the world," she still maintained a friendship with two of her girlfriends from her hometown.

Three months ago, when her university studies began, she found an apartment with other students. The freedom of university life gave her a feeling of relief, particularly because the last year at home had been very difficult. Her father had started a relationship with a much younger woman who lived in another city and who had also just begun her first semester. He had told the patient about his girlfriend before telling his wife. In the past, her father had often threatened his wife with separation. The mother had finally forced him to make a choice, not thinking that he would actually choose to leave the family. Her father moved out just before the patient left for her studies and now lived in a city in southern Germany. Already before he moved out, her mother had been in a terrible state "worse than ever before," had behaved like "a small child," would not eat, and cried all day long. The patient had been worried that her mother would hurt herself. Much to the relief of Ms. R., her mother was currently enrolled in an inpatient psychotherapy treatment program.

Selecting a Focus

The patient grew up in a stable and wealthy environment. The atmosphere within the family was influenced by her parents' diverse cultures, character traits (liberal vs. southern-traditional), and the ongoing tensions that arose as the result of their differences. Motivation for achievement, taking responsibility, social presence and acceptance also played an important role in her upbringing. Because communication between her parents was indirect, she played the role of mediator. Early on she identified with her attentive, emotional, and easily aggrieved mother, who was kept back by the ambitious and egotistical approach to life of her father. The patient attempted to emulate her father and fought for his approval.

Ms. R.'s anorexia began shortly after her Grade 11 student exchange experience. It was her first separation from the parental home; her mother did not cope well with it. The subsequent detachment process (first steady boyfriend, high school graduation, the beginning of university studies) occurred under great exertion and ambivalence, taking place at the same time as her parents' various life crises. These crises culminated in their separation as well as her mother's deep depression and suicidal tendencies. The patient's developmental process was no longer in the company of her parents, as they were busy with their own emotionally stricken separation. Additional pressure was caused by the high demands she made on herself, possibly passed on to her by her parents.

The anorexic assortment of symptoms included being a mediator for her parents; she combined her father's "youth craze" with her mother's depression and loss of appetite.

Structural foci: Affect experience and affect differentiation, regulation of self-worth, detachment.

Beginning Phase of Therapy

After the first two sessions, used mostly for the diagnostic interview, the patient presented herself as needy and sad. She reported that the sessions exposed and disturbed her past interpretations of events and that she was not sure if she was strong enough to face her inner demons. She also felt that she needed the anorexic thoughts because she could not tolerate feeling alone or sad. At the same time, she felt helpless being stuck in a life where anorexia nervosa took up such a large part of her personality.

Although during the first 4 weeks of treatment, measures were taken to relieve the patient's stress (such as only asking her to maintain her current weight), Ms. R. lost almost 1 kg (2.2 lb) for "unexplainable reasons." After the 15th session she was able to regain her initial weight. She often forgot to bring her weight curve to the sessions, and when she did have it, consistent entries were lacking. Also, she continually forgot to read the nutrition guidelines. Given the patient's neediness in conjunction with her symptoms of depression, it remained challenging in the first third of therapy to repeatedly outline and defend the therapy setting guidelines and discuss the anorexic symptoms without becoming enmeshed in a power struggle with the patient and not to affront the patient with the interpretation that she was being consumed by her anorexia nervosa.

Supportive interventions that recognized her developmental achievements and burdens in life elicited emotional reactions in the patient – almost more affect than she could take. In these situations, she reacted defensively with anorexic symptoms and remained withdrawn in the following session until a link could be made to her fear of dependence and helplessness.

Gradually, Ms. R. engaged in exploring her anorexic symptoms and began communicating her ideas. She differentiated between the little angel representing her healthy sensibility and the little devil that was synonymous with the "anorexic feeling." She noticed that the thoughts about eating occurred not only when she was feeling sad or lonely, but also during feelings of anger, listlessness, and disappointment. She recognized that the anorexic thoughts kept her from an adequate examination of her current problem. She questioned whether or not the little devil was actually more of a "scaredy-cat" that needed her understanding and comfort. She expressed feelings of self-doubt and fear of disappointing others. She began to acknowledge her own striving for achievement, perfectionism, and fear of trying something new step by step, instead of always demanding an instantaneous answer of herself. Eventually, Ms. R. was able to divulge how difficult (and ultimately prohibited) it was for her to talk about embarrassing details in her life, and she expressed her fear of a (never-ending) gain in weight that could possibly lead to her becoming "fat as a pig." She had to reassure herself that ultimately she had the power to decide and choose her eating behavior. She began to follow the nutrition guidelines after this realization.

In the course of therapy, the patient was able to adjust to her new hometown and university studies. She acquired new social contacts and acquired a new life outside of her family. This development boosted her self-confidence but also rekindled fears of possibly disappointing her new friends. Her mother was discharged from the clinic, and her father's girlfriend became pregnant. This allowed the patient to take a new view of her family situation. Her wish for everything to be like it was in the past appeared increasingly unrealistic and unattractive to her. The patient's relationship behavior took center stage, and a family session was prepared. A weight goal of 51.5 kg (113.5 lb; BMI 18.5 kg/m^2) and a weekly gain of 400 g (0.9 lb) was agreed upon.

Middle Phase of Therapy

Ms. R. showed intense fear leading up to the family session: fear that her mother might collapse into an episode of depression and that her father, who never admitted his own failings, would ask questions. She felt guilty because she was her father's confidant and was afraid of having her "cover blown" and then being discarded and left all alone, or of having to again assume the old role of mediator between her parents. Furthermore, the patient began to analyze the role anorexia played in her life and what she could lose by relinquishing the illness. The anorexic disorder secured her parents' attention and caregiving; she was worried that if she recovered, her parents would become consumed with their "wasteful divorce war." The fear of losing her father's attention was especially bothersome. Currently, he visited her weekly and took her to expensive restaurants. Giving up her anorexia nervosa not only meant losing a pillar of her day-to-day life, but also meant confessing to having made a mistake and having failed when, generally speaking, she succeeded easily at things. She did not know who she would be if she no longer filled the role of the "showcase daughter." At the same time, she was beginning to feel angry about this role and the limitations anorexia nervosa placed on her.

Ms. R.'s mother agreed to the family session with the provision that her husband would not attend. This was a relief to the patient. Her brother was also not able to attend as he had responsibilities at his boarding school. During the entire family session, the patient cried and made clear that she only wanted to discuss the therapeutic framework of her treatment and not the specific elements of her family conflicts and relationship constellations. Her mother conveyed a spirited, optimistic, forward-looking image of herself. She felt that everyone's life would go on, just that her daughter "was stuck" and "must have taken the brunt of the catastrophe." She did concede the patient's role as translator and mediator within the family and that she needed her, but also understood that her daughter needed to achieve independence. Her mother was worried that the patient would always be starving herself in future when problems came up. Even with therapeutic support, Ms. R. was barely able to voice her own needs and wishes to her mother. At this juncture, a provisional stop signal (i.e., a verbal indicator or code word) was introduced that could be used when one of them would feel overworked and pressured by the other.

In the meetings following the family session, the patient reported an increase in sadness – but also a feeling of angry vitality. She brought up day-to-day situations in which she felt overlooked and misunderstood and recognized her tendency to quickly withdraw from situations. She agonized over problems in order to not burden others or put herself in a bad light. Individual episodes, even in the here-and-now of the client–therapist relationship, were able to be closely analyzed. The patient was motivated to try out new behavior.

Ms. R. began eating more and steadily gained weight. These elicited feelings of both pride and fear. Sporadic binge eating attacks occurred. She began to menstruate again.

Closing Phase of Therapy

During the closing phase of therapy, numerous external changes and challenges took place. The patient completed an important exam in her studies, shared an apartment with new friends, and felt like she had finally "arrived in her new hometown." Her father checked into an inpatient "burnout" treatment program and resigned from his job in order to start up a freelance company. His girlfriend gave birth to twins. Her mother began a new position at work and began a relationship with a man, who unfortunately passed away shortly thereafter.

Initially Ms. R. avoided speaking about the conclusion of therapy. However, she began to disregard therapy agreements (e.g., by not coming to a session, arriving at the last minute, or leaving early). This was discussed with her and brought to her attention in terms of her relationship dynamics. Further, her feelings alternated between pride for her newly acquired skills, fear concerning new situations, and anger toward the therapist for having, as she framed it, "instigated all of this, just to abandon her." Anorexic eating behavior reoccurred on individual days, coupled with sporadic binge eating, but the patient was promptly able to control this independently. In the course of balancing the joint experiences of the patient and therapist, successes and goals were outlined (e.g., BMI at the end of therapy: 17.9 kg/m²). For the patient a pivotal aspect of therapy was the therapist's expressed trust in her healthy development and the implied permission to attend to her "normal life." Furthermore, she reported that an important step for her was contrasting her alliance with anorexia nervosa with her alliance with the therapist and also, that by internalizing the therapeutic alliance, she was able to use it as an inner advisor, even outside the therapy sessions.

Acknowledgments

We would like to thank Miriam Komo-Lang for her contributions to these case studies.

6 Efficacy

6.1 Research Background

The scientific evaluation of treatment plans for anorexia nervosa is difficult because the illness raises various therapeutic and methodological obstacles that can occur when treating anorexic patients under the parameters of a study. The realization of a clinical study concerning anorexics poses challenges. The following are examples of typical obstacles:

The realization of a clinical study concerning anorexia nervosa poses challenges

1. In the classical research design regarding the efficacy of a treatment, patients are usually randomly assigned to either the intervention or control group (i.e., RCT = randomized controlled trial). Since the reality of anorexia nervosa is such that medical complications are often imminent (caused by a dangerously low BMI), a control group that makes a patient either wait for treatment or receive an inadequately supportive therapy is not a feasible option. Such studies are currently viewed as unethical. Consequently, previous studies have, at times, resulted in a high rate of premature termination in the control groups.

2. The illness has a low prevalence rate. Recruiting enough patients for an RCT is expensive and requires the participation of several study centers.

3. Many anorexia nervosa patients are ambivalent about inpatient or outpatient treatment. Due to this reluctance, recruitment for an RCT can be difficult. Then again, there is the possibility of a high dropout rate. This can bias the results of the study.

4. In the course of assessing outpatient treatment, and because of severity of illness, physical complications can occur that require admission to inpatient treatment. Findings from previous research demonstrate that such hospitalizations can lead to high dropout rates. Thus, for example, Halmi and others (2005) suggested that study protocols for RCTs regarding outpatient therapy of anorexic patients should allow for hospitalization for a predefined, limited time period (Halmi et al., 2005).

5. To date it remains unclear what the specific components of therapy are that lead to recovery for anorexic patients. We

know from clinical practice that specific components of therapy (e.g., the weight contract and the focus on weight gain) are important elements of treatment. However, even with therapy, the time to recovery can be protracted (a mean 6 years; Herzog et al., 1997); about 20% of patients develop a chronic form of anorexia nervosa with severe physical and psychological complications.

To date, only marginal evidence exists regarding the efficacy of psychotherapy for anorexia nervosa; this is due to the fact that the abovementioned challenges have produced limited evidence. In a recent review, Brockmeyer, Friederich, and Schmidt (2017) were able to identify 13 RCTs regarding outpatient therapy of adult anorexia nervosa patients.

Dare, Eisler, Russell, Treasure, and Dodge (2001) demonstrated that the three specialized forms of therapy (focal psychoanalytical, cognitive analytical, and family-oriented therapy) outmatched the routine treatment given by resident doctors in psychiatric units that primarily monitored weight gain. Pike, Walsh, Vitousek, Wilson, and Bauer (2003), using relapse rates as the measurement, were able to verify that CBT was more successful than nutrition counseling. Admittedly, this study resulted in a dropout rate of 73% in the control group; as such, the results cannot be considered valid. In contrast to these findings, McIntosh et al. (2005) found that patients who participated in a control group – that is, specialist supportive clinical management (SSCM) – showed better results for global outcomes compared with patients who took part in interpersonal therapy (IPT) or CBT (McIntosh et al., 2005); however, the long-term follow-up of this trial did not support the superiority of any one of the therapies (Carter et al., 2011).

Another trial of 63 severely chronic anorexia patients found that at the end of treatment, the results for CBT were not better than those for supportive control treatment (Touyz et al., 2013). Furthermore, a novel anorexia nervosa–specific outpatient treatment, the Maudsley model of anorexia nervosa therapy for adults (MANTRA), was tested against SSCM in two separate studies (Schmidt et al., 2012; Schmidt et al., 2015), while in another study SSCM, MANTRA, and enhanced cognitive behavior therapy (CBT-E) were compared (Byrne et al., 2017). Although MANTRA, SSCM, and CBT-E showed no significant differences with respect to overall outcome (Schmidt et al., 2012; Schmidt et al., 2015), MANTRA, as compared with SSCM, was more effective in patients with a severe illness.

To date, only marginal evidence exists for the efficacy of psychotherapy for anorexia nervosa

In summary, the evidence for the treatment of adult outpatients suffering from anorexia nervosa is increasing. In terms of therapeutic change and long-term global outcomes, some advantages have been reported for specific treatments, such as focal psychodynamic therapy (FPT), IPT, CBT-E, MANTRA, over treatment as usual or SSCM (Carter et al., 2011; Schmidt et al., 2015; Zipfel et al., 2014). However, no specific approach has been proven to be superior with respect to weight gain (Brockmeyer et al., 2017).

It should be noted, however, that all of the cited studies used relatively small samples, and the length of treatment was a mean 20 sessions; this is very short for such a complex illness. The question remains, therefore, whether or not these studies were unable to prove treatment success because of the small number of cases or because of an insufficient number of therapy sessions. However, between 2007 and 2011, a large multicenter RCT regarding outpatient therapy of anorexia nervosa was carried out, the results of which were published in Zipfel et al. (2014). This study will be described in detail in the following section.

6.2   The ANTOP Study

Within the framework of the Anorexia Nervosa Treatment of Outpatients (ANTOP) study, the efficacy of a manual-based and disease-oriented psychodynamic or CBT approach (Fairburn, 2008) to anorexia nervosa was investigated and compared with the treatment-as-usual approach.

6.2.1   Design and Participants

The ANTOP study was a multicenter RCT of ambulant psychotherapy. In total, 242 patients with anorexia nervosa were included in the study at 10 different university centers. Participation in the psychotherapy study required that patients were of age and female, with a BMI between 15 kg/m² and 18.5 kg/m², and showing either the full syndrome or subsyndromal anorexia nervosa (subsyndromal, according to the DSM-IV criteria, is defined as missing one diagnostic criterion of anorexia nervosa). Exclusion criteria were the prescribed use of neuroleptics and the presentation of borderline or bipolar disorder. Further details can be found in the publication of the study protocol (Wild et al., 2009).

The ANTOP study was a multicenter RCT of ambulant psychotherapy

After patients had been included in the study, they were randomly assigned to one of its three arms – that is, FPT, CBT-E, or optimized treatment as usual (TAU-O). In the FPT and CBT-E groups, each participant received a disease-oriented, manual-based psychotherapy consisting of 40 sessions. The FPT program corresponded to the procedure described in this manual. The CBT-E program followed the program of Fairburn and Beglin (2008). The control (TAU-O) group, however, was given a list of qualified therapists with the recommendation that they participate in an outpatient therapy.

The length of treatment for both of the manual-based therapy programs was set for 10 months (i.e., 40 sessions). The primary outcome for the efficacy of treatment was BMI measured at the end of treatment (10 months after randomization). Follow-up measurements were conducted at 3 months and then 1 year posttreatment to determine long-term effects and the sustainability of the therapy influence.

At the beginning of the study, the average BMI of the 242 patients included was 16.7 kg/m²; close to three fourths of the patients (71%) had a BMI < 17.5 kg/m². There were no significant variances in starting weight for the three branches of treatment. Furthermore, one half of patients showed anorexia nervosa of the binge-eating/purging type.

Almost one fourth of patients (22.3%) dropped out in the first 10 months of treatment. Dropout was defined as the fact that patients were not available for further measurements. At the 1-year follow-up, the dropout rate had risen to 30.1%. The proportion of patients who prematurely terminated the two manualized arms of therapy was 26.3%, which is relatively low for this disorder. Further characteristics can be found in the main publication of the study (Zipfel et al., 2014).

6.2.2   Weight Gain and Recovery

Figure 4 illustrates patients' weight gain across the three treatment groups and across all three time point measurements.

Figure 4 demonstrates that, as time progressed, the average weight of the patients increased across all three treatment arms. However, the primary analysis of the BMI data yielded no significant differences between the three treatment groups at any specific point in time.

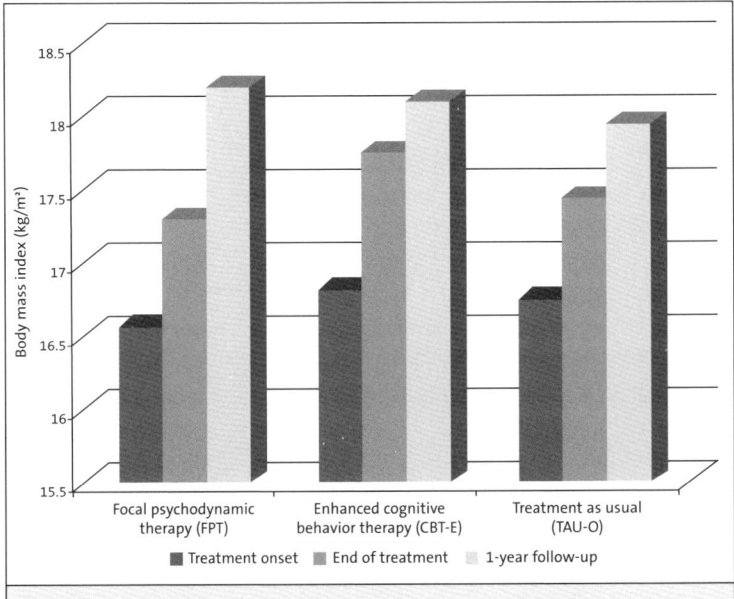

Figure 4
Body mass index at the beginning, end of treatment, and at 1-year follow-up for each of three treatment groups in the Anorexia Nervosa Treatment of Outpatients (ANTOP) study. The TAU-O group was the control. Based on Zipfel et al. (2014).

At the conclusion of therapy, and at the 1-year follow-up, based on BMI criteria and external evaluation of symptoms (using the Psychiatric Status Rating Scale, PSR; Herzog, Sacks, et al., 1993), patients were classified into three groups: those with a good result (*remission*), a moderate result (*partial remission*), and a poor result (*full syndrome of anorexia nervosa*). Immediately after the conclusion of treatment, patients in all three groups did not differ in the global evaluation. However, at 1-year follow-up, the FPT group had significantly more patients showing remission than the control group (35.2% vs. 12.5%). Figure 5 shows the global outcomes for patients across all three measurement points:

A further analysis of the outpatient dosage of therapy sessions resulted in no differences between the three treatment groups. However, data showed that at the time of the 1-year follow-up, the patients in the control group had significantly more inpatient admissions than the patients assigned to the FPT group (Zipfel et al., 2014).

Within the framework of the psychodynamic psychotherapy, one third of patients were able to reach remission.

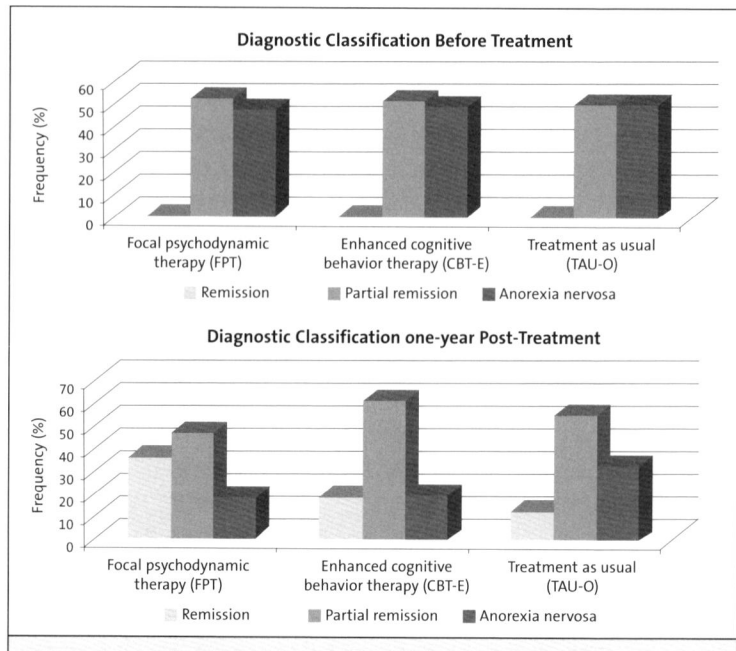

Figure 5
Global outcomes of therapy, differentiated according to three treatment groups in the Anorexia Nervosa Treatment of Outpatients (ANTOP) study. The TAU-O group was the control.
Based on Zipfel et al. (2014).

6.2.3   Predictors of Outcome

Research on the predictors of disease outcome is largely based on observational studies and, to a lesser extent, on interventional studies. Both observational and interventional studies showed consistently that a higher BMI, a lower age, and a shorter duration of illness at study onset were linked to a more favorable outcome. With regard to psychosocial predictors the findings are less clear. However, psychosocial factors observed to be associated with a favorable disease outcome are purging behavior, high self-esteem, severe eating disorder psychopathology, high treatment motivation, and lack of depressive comorbidity (Vall & Wade, 2015).

In the ANTOP study, planned as an interventional study in outpatients, lifetime mental comorbidity was assessed with the Structured Clinical Interview for DSM-IV Axis I disorders as the gold standard. The following predictors of treatment response were confirmed: The strongest positive predictor for BMI and recovery at 1-year follow-up was a higher baseline BMI in patients; conversely, negative predictors of treatment outcome (BMI, recovery at 1-year follow-up) were a more advanced age at baseline, a duration of illness > 6 years, and comorbid lifetime (including current) depression (or low self-esteem) at baseline (Wild et al., 2016). Furthermore, depression and self-esteem were highly intercorrelated, making self-esteem redundant when depression was considered as predictor in the model. Anxiety disorders including obsessive-compulsive disorders, eating disorder psychopathology, and subtype of disorder showed no significant prediction of treatment outcome (Wild et al., 2016).

Thus, the research into psychological predictors that was focused on in the ANTOP study was able to underline the relevance of comorbid depression in determining disease severity. This supports the manual's therapeutic approach of centering on self-esteem problems and depressive experiences from the beginning of therapy (see Section 4.4.5: Focusing in on Self-Esteem Problems and Depressive Experiences). Furthermore, affective comorbidities were closely related to body image dissatisfaction at all stages of the 10-month treatment, while body image perception at baseline predicted depressive symptomatology at the 1-year follow-up. The findings suggest therefore that focusing on self-worth and depressive symptomatology should also include the targeted therapeutic approaches that address body image disturbances (Junne et al., 2016).

Additionally, social predictors that are dependent on family, partnership, education, and the occupational situation of the patient were analyzed. The family dimension included the following variables: moving out of the parental home, parental separation or illness, the loss of a parent, and the specific position within the sibling order. Despite the therapeutic relevance of the unsuccessful detachment process that anorexia nervosa patients often show, the overall variables of family and partnership had no predictive value for weight-related treatment outcome in the ANTOP study. Likewise, education and occupation showed no significant prediction for treatment outcome (Teufel et al., 2017).

6.2.4   Therapeutic Process and Outcome

Patients with anorexia nervosa are characterized by an avoidance of negative emotions and show marked difficulties in the regulation of their emotion (see also Section 2.1: Psychodynamic Understanding). However, it remains unclear whether the increased emotional processing during in-session and between-session psychotherapy is connected to a better outcome at the end of treatment and at 1-year follow-up. The ANTOP study also investigated whether the heightened expression of negative emotions could be associated with a favorable outcome.

During the ANTOP study, therapy sessions were audio recorded. Transcripts of the audio files of an early therapy session (from sessions 4–15), middle sessions (16–32), and late sessions (33–40) were created. Session selection in each treatment phase was based on the highest-rated session quality as selected by the Short-Inventory for Single Psychotherapy and Counselling (Krampen & Wald, 2001). In addition to the above, one of the initial three sessions was chosen in the same manner. The selected transcripts were then analyzed with computerized text analysis software to assess the patient's verbal expression of emotions. In addition to assessing the total number of emotional words, the software differentiated between positive and negative emotional words. Across all treatment phases, the verbal expression of negative emotional words was highest in the middle phase compared with the early and late treatment phases. There were no significant differences between FPT and CBT-E in this regard.

Hierarchical regression analyses were used to assess the relationship between the quantitative analyses of verbal data and BMI at the end of treatment and at 1-year follow-up. The a priori hypothesis (i.e., that more numerous negative emotional expressions would predict weight gain) was confirmed, since the number of negative rather than positive emotional words expressed during the middle phase was positively correlated with weight gain at the end of treatment and at 1-year follow-up. For the latter, the findings fell short of being significant. The findings were specific to the middle treatment phase, as neither negative or positive emotions in the initial, early, or late treatment phases predicted the BMI at end of treatment or 1-year follow-up. Furthermore, the findings were independent of treatment condition (FPT or CBT-E), duration of illness, anorexia subtype, and BMI at treatment onset.

The findings indicate that therapists should actively focus on increasing emotional expression in anorexia nervosa patients, especially during the middle treatment phase (Friederich et al., 2017).

Research variables should cover both time periods due to the fact that the therapeutic process takes place not only within but also between therapy sessions. In outpatient psychotherapy, clients spend much more time outside the therapy setting than with their therapist. Therefore, therapeutic process research in outpatients should include how the clients experience and process outpatient psychotherapy between sessions – that is, intersession processes (ISPs). To study ISPs, participants were asked to complete the Intersession Experience Questionnaire (Hartmann et al., 2016; Orlinsky, Geller, Tarragona, & Farber, 1993) before each of the 40 psychotherapy sessions. The ISP Questionnaire includes the following dimensions: (a) intensity of ISP (i.e., frequency and duration of thinking about therapy and therapist), (b) the context in which the ISP that differentiates between the emotive, problem solving, and dreaming–drowsy states arise, (c) thought content (including relationship fantasies) that recreate the therapeutic dialogue and apply therapeutic learning, and (d) the emotional tone of thoughts about therapy, that allow for the differentiation between positive and negative emotions.

The treatment conditions FPT and CBT-E showed surprisingly similar ISPs. In the middle phase of treatment, differences between treatment conditions were found pertaining to both therapy-related negative emotions and memories. In the FPT condition, negative emotions in the middle phase appeared to be part of the psychotherapeutic process and associated with a good outcome, whereas in the CBT-E, this was not the case (Zeeck et al., 2016). Furthermore, the findings do not support the hypothesis that the psychotherapeutic process is more successful if between sessions there were a greater frequency of therapy-related thoughts, memories, and expression of emotions. Instead, the findings indicate that the frequency of processing should lie within an optimal range in the course of therapy progression and depends specifically on the treatment phase (Hartmann et al., 2016; Zeeck et al., 2016).

In summary, process-outcome research of the ANTOP study underscores the relevance of affective–emotional processing in the psychodynamic treatment of anorexia nervosa patients. In addition, the findings show that affective–emotional processing in the middle phase of treatment is of the utmost importance for a favorable outcome. The middle phase of therapy usually constitutes the most intense emotional phase in psychotherapy. When embedded in the therapy timeline, this indicates that patients usually need to familiarize themselves with their therapist as well as the characteristics of treatment during the early phase of therapy; they should not be confronted prematurely with negative emotions and interpersonal experiences until later in the therapeutic process. Similarly, during the later phase of treatment, the patients must learn to gradually loosen the therapeutic bond and get back to autonomy – an autonomy that focuses on skills other than expressing their emotions. In the course of a comprehensive overview of the progression of therapy, it becomes clear why the scrutiny of emotions occurs most intensely during the middle phase.

6.2.5   Cost-of-Illness and Cost-Effectiveness Analyses

Anorexia nervosa is characteristically of a chronic nature that requires recurrent treatment. Patients have an extremely high rate of being in need of inpatient treatment; they have the longest median length of stay of all mental disorders (Thompson et al., 2004). Further direct costs result from outpatient treatment, pharmaceuticals, social services, and out-of-pocket expenses that are paid for by the patient and their family. Apart from direct costs, indirect costs arise because of sick leave, reduced productivity at the workplace due to absenteeism, and disability. In summary, the findings indicate that the cost of illness for anorexia nervosa is substantial; however, previous studies have shown heterogeneous findings. The implication is, therefore, that currently there are no studies that provide a comprehensive estimate of costs (Stuhldreher et al., 2012).

In the ANTOP study, the utilization of health care services and on-the-job productivity loss, as well as indirect determinants of costs, were assessed at baseline (i.e., before the beginning of treatment) for the previous 3 months before treatment. Mean 3-month direct and indirect costs per patient totaled the equivalent of US$ 6,584 (€ 5,866). Direct costs accounted for 57% of the total. The majority of the costs were the result of inpatient treatment. Determinants of direct costs for outpatients were noted to be highest for patients of the binge-eating/purging type, with an illness duration of more than 6 years, and by patients suffering from a comorbid mental disorder. Findings indicated that the costs of illness were high, particularly because additional inpatient treatment of the assessed patients was necessary (Stuhldreher et al., 2015).

Furthermore, the cost-effectiveness of outpatient therapies for treating anorexia nervosa was analyzed in conjunction with the ANTOP trial. Cost-effectiveness was determined for the 10 months of outpatient treatment together with the 12-month follow-up period. With regard to recovery and direct costs, FPT proved cost-effective when compared with CBT-E and TAU-O. For additional details, interested readers are referred to Egger et al. (2016).

6.2.6 Summary

To date, the ANTOP study is the largest RCT to examine the efficacy of outpatient therapy for adult anorexia nervosa patients. The study sets itself apart not only by the size of the sample, but also because of the comparatively low dropout rate and the specifically tailored study protocol that allowed for an inpatient admission for a period not exceeding 4 weeks. With this relatively large sample (representative for German eating disorder centers), we became aware of the fact that average BMI can improve significantly over the course of a 10-month outpatient program.

The average BMI increase across the three treatment groups at the time of the 1-year follow-up was as follows: for FPT, 1.64 kg/m²; CBT-E, 1.30 kg/m²; control group, 1.22 kg/m². However, the figures for mean weight gain were small, indicating how difficult it is for patients suffering from anorexia nervosa to gain weight.

The two specialized therapies (FPT and CBT-E) did not differ from the control group when BMI was compared at the end of therapy. However, it should be taken into account that the patients in the control group received a comparable therapy dosage and were free to choose the therapy program of their liking; the established therapists were often more experienced than the therapists who conducted the manualized treatment. This implies that the treatment in the control group was comparatively intensive, which could have influenced the nonsignificant differences in BMI between the treatment groups.

With regard to the global assessment of recovery at the 1-year follow-up, an advantage was seen for patients who had participated in the FPT group when compared with the control group. In addition to BMI, the global outcome was defined as the secondary, clinically relevant outcome criteria. A further advantage of the FPT group, when compared with the control group, was found in the lower number of inpatient admissions. Given the differences in frequency of inpatient treatment across the treatment conditions, FPT proved cost-effective as compared with CBT-E and TAU-O (control).

Secondary analyses of data from the ANTOP study underscore the relevance of depressive comorbidity and self-esteem in the prediction of outcomes and the importance of affective-emotional processing during the middle phase of treatment for a favorable outcome. Findings support a phased (early, middle, late) course of treatment, each with its own therapeutic challenges. The findings also suggest that the middle phase of therapy can serve as the main working segment for addressing affective–emotional processing. Furthermore, the therapist should be sensitive to the patient's resources and should find the optimal range of affective–emotional confrontations, as confrontation levels that are too high seem to be associated with an unproductive or otherwise problematic processes. Nevertheless, outcome prediction and process-outcome research of the ANTOP study have made important contributions to improve our understanding of potential mechanisms of change that could inform future treatment programs.

Taken as a whole, the results of the ANTOP study allow for the inference that physically stable anorexia nervosa patients with a BMI $\geq$ 15.0 kg/m² can be successfully treated in an outpatient therapy program.

Physically stable adult patients with a BMI $\geq$ 15.0 kg/m² can be treated in an outpatient setting

7 References

Agras, W. S., Brandt, H. A., Bulik, C. M., Dolan-Sewell, R., Fairburn, C. G., Halmi, K. A., . . . Wilfley, D. E. (2004). Report of the National Institutes of Health workshop on overcoming barriers to treatment research in anorexia nervosa. *International Journal of Eating Disorders, 35*(4), 509–521. https://doi.org/10.1002/eat.10261

American Psychiatric Association. (2006). *Practice guideline for the treatment of patients with eating disorders* (3rd ed.). Arlington, VA: American Psychiatric Publishing. Retrieved from http://psychiatryonline.org/pb/assets/raw/sitewide/practice_guidelines/guidelines/eatingdisorders.pdf

American Psychiatric Association. (2009). *Diagnostic and statistical manual of mental disorders: DSM-IV-TR* (4th ed., text revision). Arlington, VA: Author.

American Psychiatric Association. (2013). *Diagnostic and statistical manual of mental disorders: DSM-5* (5th ed.). Arlington, VA: American Psychiatric Publishing. http://doi.org/10.1176/appi.books.9780890425596

Arcelus, J., Mitchell, A. J., Wales, J., & Nielsen, S. (2011). Mortality rates in patients with anorexia nervosa and other eating disorders: A meta-analysis of 36 studies. *Archives of General Psychiatry, 68*(7), 724–731. http://doi.org/10.1001/archgenpsychiatry.2011.74

Association of the Medical Societies in Germany. (2011). *S3 Guideline: Diagnostic and therapy of eating disorders*. Retrieved from www.awmf.org/leitlinien/detail/ll/051-026.html

Bartholomew, K., Kwong, M. J., & Hart, S. D. (2001). Attachment. In W. J. Livesley (Ed.), *Handbook of personality disorders: Theory, research, and treatment* (pp. 196–230). New York, NY: Guilford Press.

Bers, S. A., Besser, A., Harpaz-Rotem, I., & Blatt, S. J. (2013). An empirical exploration of the dynamics of anorexia nervosa: Representations of self, mother, and father. *Psychoanalytic Psychology, 30*(2), 188–209. http://doi.org/10.1037/a0032512

Berkman, N. D., Lohr, K. N., Bulik, C. M. (2007). Outcomes of eating disorders. A systematic review of the literature. *The International Journal of Eating Disorders, 40*(4), 293–309. http://doi.org/10.1002/eat.20369

Boris, H. N. (1984). The problem of anorexia nervosa. *International Journal of Psycho-Analysis, 65*(Pt 3), 315–322.

Brockmeyer, T., Bents, H., Holtforth, M. G., Pfeiffer, N., Herzog, W., & Friederich, H.-C. (2012). Specific emotion regulation impairments in major depression and anorexia nervosa. *Psychiatry Research, 200*(2–3), 550–553. http://doi.org/10.1016/j.psychres.2012.07.009

Brockmeyer, T., Friederich, H. C., & Schmidt, U. (2017). Advances in the treatment of anorexia nervosa: A review of established and emerging interventions. *Psychological Medicine, 11*, 1–37. https://doi.org/10.1017/S0033291717002604

Brockmeyer, T., Grosse Holtforth, M., Bents, H., Herzog, W., & Friederich, H.-C. (2013). Lower body weight is associated with less negative emotions in sad autobiographical memories of patients with anorexia nervosa. *Psychiatry Research, 210*(2), 548–552. http://doi.org/10.1016/j.psychres. 2013.06.024

Bruch, H. (1962). Perceptual and conceptual disturbances in anorexia nervosa. *Psychosomatic Medicine, 24,* 187–194. http://doi.org/10.1097/00006842-196203000-00009

Bruch, H. (1978). *The golden cage: The enigma of anorexia nervosa.* Cambridge, MA: Harvard University Press.

Bulik, C. M., Kleiman, S. C., & Yilmaz, Z. (2016). Genetic epidemiology of eating disorders. *Current Opinion in Psychiatry, 29*(6), 383–388. http://doi.org/10.1097/YCO.0000000000000275

Bulik, C. M., Sullivan, P. F., Tozzi, F., Furberg, H., Lichtenstein, P., & Pedersen, N. L. (2006). Prevalence, heritability, and prospective risk factors for anorexia nervosa. *Archives of General Psychiatry, 63*(3), 305–312. http://doi.org/10.1001/archpsyc.63.3.305

Byrne, S., Wade, T., Hay, P., Touyz, S., Fairburn, C. G., Treasure, J., . . . Crosby, R. D. (2017). A randomised controlled trial of three psychological treatments for anorexia nervosa. *Psychological Medicine,* 1–11. http://doi.org/10.1017/S0033291717001349

Caglar-Nazali, H. P., Corfield, F., Cardi, V., Ambwani, S., Leppanen, J., Olabintan, O., . . . Treasure, J. (2014). A systematic review and meta-analysis of 'Systems for Social Processes' in eating disorders. *Neuroscience and Biobehavioral Reviews, 42,* 55–92. http://doi.org/10.1016/j.neubiorev.2013.12.002

Carter, F. A., Jordan, J., McIntosh, V. V. W., Luty, S. E., McKenzie, J. M., Frampton, C. M. A., . . . Joyce, P. R. (2011). The long-term efficacy of three psychotherapies for anorexia nervosa: A randomized, controlled trial. *International Journal of Eating Disorders, 44*(7), 647–654. https://doi.org/10.1002/eat.20879

Cassin, S. E., & von Ranson, K. M. (2005). Personality and eating disorders: A decade in review. *Clinical Psychology Review, 25*(7), 895–916. http://doi.org/10.1016/j.cpr.2005.04.012

Cervera, S., Lahortiga, F., Martinez-Gonzalez, M. A., Gual, P., de Irala-Estevez, J., & Alonso, Y. (2003). Neuroticism and low self-esteem as risk factors for incident eating disorders in a prospective cohort study. *International Journal of Eating Disorders, 33*(3), 271–280. https://doi.org/10.1002/eat.10147

Clarkin, J. F., Fonagy, P., & Gabbard, G. O. (Eds.). (2010). *Psychodynamic psychotherapy for personality disorders: A clinical handbook* (1st ed.). Washington, DC: American Psychiatric Publishing.

Cloninger, C. R., Svrakic, D. M., & Przybeck, T. R. (1993). A psychobiological model of temperament and character. *Archives of General Psychiatry, 50*(12), 975–990. http://doi.org/10.1001/archpsyc.1993.01820240059008

Cnattingius, S., Hultman, C. M., Dahl, M., & Sparen, P. (1999). Very preterm birth, birth trauma, and the risk of anorexia nervosa among girls. *Archives of General Psychiatry, 56*(7), 634–638. http://doi.org/10.1001/archpsyc.56.7.634

Culbert, K. M., Racine, S. E., & Klump, K. L. (2015). Research review: What we have learned about the causes of eating disorders – A synthesis of sociocultural, psychological, and biological research. *Journal of Child Psychology and Psychiatry, and Allied Disciplines, 56*(11), 1141–1164. https://doi.org/10.1111/jcpp.12441

Currin, L., Schmidt, U., Treasure, J., & Jick, H. (2005). Time trends in eating disorder incidence. *British Journal of Psychiatry, 186,* 132–135. http://doi.org/10.1192/bjp.186.2.132

Dare, C., Eisler, I., Russell, G., Treasure, J., & Dodge, L. (2001). Psychological therapies for adults with anorexia nervosa: Randomised controlled trial of out-patient treatments. *British Journal of Psychiatry, 178,* 216–221. http://doi.org/10.1192/bjp.178.3.216

Duncan, L., Yilmaz, Z., Gaspar, H., Walters, R., Goldstein, J., Anttila, V., . . . Bulik, C. M. (2017). Significant locus and metabolic genetic correlations revealed in genome-wide association study of anorexia nervosa. *American Journal of Psychiatry, 174*(9), 850–858. https://doi.org/10.1176/appi.ajp.2017.16121402

Eddy, K. T., Hennessey, M., & Thompson-Brenner, H. (2007). Eating pathology in East African women: The role of media exposure and globalization. *Journal of Nervous and Mental Disease, 195*(3), 196–202. http://doi.org/10.1097/01.nmd.0000243922.49394.7d

Egan, S. J., Wade, T. D., & Shafran, R. (2011). Perfectionism as a transdiagnostic process: A clinical review. *Clinical Psychology Review, 31*(2), 203–212. http://doi.org/10.1016/j.cpr.2010.04.009

Egger, N., Wild, B., Zipfel, S., Junne, F., Konnopka, A., Schmidt, U., . . . König, H.-H. (2016). Cost-effectiveness of focal psychodynamic therapy and enhanced cognitive-behavioural therapy in out-patients with anorexia nervosa. *Psychological Medicine, 46*(16), 3291–3301. http://doi.org/10.1017/S0033291716002002

Fairburn, C. G. (Ed.). (2008). *Cognitive behavior therapy and eating disorders.* New York, NY: Guilford Press.

Fairburn, C. G., & Beglin, S. J. (2008). Eating Disorder Examination Questionnaire. In C. G. Fairburn (Ed.), *Cognitive behavior therapy and eating disorders.* New York, NY: Guilford Press.

Fairburn, C. G., & Cooper, Z. (1987). The Eating Disorder Examination: A semistructured interview for the assessment of the specific psychopathology of eating disorders. *International Journal of Eating Disorders, 6*(1), 1–8. http://doi.org/10.1002/1098-108X(198701)6:1<1::AID-EAT2260060102>3.0.CO;2-9

Favaro, A., Tenconi, E., & Santonastaso, P. (2006). Perinatal factors and the risk of developing anorexia nervosa and bulimia nervosa. *Archives of General Psychiatry, 63*(1), 82–88. http://doi.org/10.1001/archpsyc.63.1.82

First, M., Williams, J. B., Karg, R. S., & Spitzer, R. L. (2016). *Structured clinical interview for DSM-5 disorders – clinician version (SCID-5-cv).* Arlington, VA: American Psychiatric Publishing.

Fishman, H. C. (2004). *Enduring change in eating disorders: Interventions with long-term results.* New York, NY: Brunner-Routledge.

Friederich, H.-C., Brockmeyer, T., Wild, B., Resmark, G., de Zwaan, M., Dinkel, A., . . . Herzog, W. (2017). Emotional expression predicts treatment outcome in focal psychodynamic and cognitive behavioural therapy for anorexia nervosa: Findings from the ANTOP study. *Psychotherapy and Psychosomatics, 86*(2), 108–110. https://doi.org/10.1159/000453582

Friederich, H.-C., Walther, S., Bendszus, M., Biller, A., Thomann, P., Zeigermann, S., . . . Herzog, W. (2012). Grey matter abnormalities within cortico-limbic-striatal circuits in acute and weight-restored anorexia nervosa patients. *Neuroimage, 59*(2), 1106–1113. http://doi.org/10.1016/j.neuroimage.2011.09.042

Friederich, H.-C., Wu, M., Simon, J. J., & Herzog, W. (2013). Neurocircuit function in eating disorders. *International Journal of Eating Disorders, 46*(5), 425–432. http://doi.org/10.1002/eat.22099

Garner, D. M. (2004). *Eating Disorder Inventory-3 (EDI™-3): Professional manual.* Lutz, FL: Psychological Assessment Resources.

Garner, D. M., & Bemis, K. M. (1982). A cognitive-behavioral approach to anorexia nervosa. *Cognitive Therapy and Research, 6*(2), 123–150. http://doi.org/10.1007/BF01183887

Garner, D. M., Olmstead, M. P., & Polivy, J. (1983). Development and validation of a multidimensional eating disorder inventory for anorexia nervosa and bulimia. *International Journal of Eating Disorders, 2*(2), 15–34. http://doi.org/10.1002/1098-108X(198321)2:2<15::AID-EAT2260020203>3.0.CO;2-6

Godart, N. T., Flament, M. F., Perdereau, F., & Jeammet, P. (2002). Comorbidity between eating disorders and anxiety disorders: A review. *International Journal of Eating Disorders, 32*(3), 253–270. http://doi.org/10.1002/eat.10096

Godart, N. T., Perdereau, F., Rein, Z., Berthoz, S., Wallier, J., Jeammet, P., & Flament, M. F. (2007). Comorbidity studies of eating disorders and mood disorders: Critical review of the literature. *Journal of Affective Disorders, 97*(1–3), 37–49. http://doi.org/10.1016/j.jad.2006.06.023

Gull, W. W. (1873). Anorexia nervosa (Apepsia hysterica, anorexia hysterical). *Clinical Society's Transaction, 874*, 22.

Habermas, T. (1994). *The history of anorexia nervosa: A medical-psychological reconstruction.* Frankfurt am Main, Germany: Fischer.

Halmi, K. A., Agras, W. S., Crow, S., Mitchell, J., Wilson, G. T., Bryson, S. W., & Kraemer, H. C. (2005). Predictors of treatment acceptance and completion in anorexia nervosa: Implications for future study designs. *Archives of General Psychiatry, 62*(7), 776–781. https://doi.org/10.1001/archpsyc.62.7.776

Hartmann, A., Zeeck, A., Herzog, W., Wild, B., de Zwaan, M., Herpertz, S., . . . Zipfel, S. (2016). The intersession process in psychotherapy for anorexia nervosa: Characteristics and relation to outcome. *Journal of Clinical Psychology, 72*(9), 861–879. http://doi.org/10.1002/jclp.22293

Herzog, D. B., Sacks, N. R., Keller, M. B., Lavori, P. W., von Ranson, K. B., & Gray, H. M. (1993). Patterns and predictors of recovery in anorexia nervosa and bulimia nervosa. *Journal of the American Academy of Child and Adolescent Psychiatry, 32*(4), 835–842. http://doi.org/10.1097/00004583-199307000-00020

Herzog, W., Kronmüller, K. T., Hartmann, M., Bergmann, G., & Kröger, F. (2000). Family perception of interpersonal behavior as a predictor in eating disorders: A prospective, six-year followup study. *Family Process, 39*(3), 359–374. http://doi.org/10.1111/j.1545-5300.2000.39307.x

Herzog, W., Minne, H., Deter, C., Leidig, G., Schellberg, D., Wuster, C., . . . Bergmann, G. (1993). Outcome of bone mineral density in anorexia nervosa patients 11.7 years after first admission. *Journal of Bone and Mineral Research, 8*(5), 597–605. https://doi.org/10.1002/jbmr.5650080511

Herzog, W., Schellberg, D., & Deter, H. C. (1997). First recovery in anorexia nervosa patients in the long-term course: A discrete-time survival analysis. *Journal of Consulting and Clinical Psychology, 65*(1), 169–177. http://doi.org/10.1037/0022-006X.65.1.169

Hudson, J. I., Hiripi, E., Pope, H. G., Jr., & Kessler, R. C. (2007). The prevalence and correlates of eating disorders in the National Comorbidity Survey Replication. *Biological Psychiatry, 61*(3), 348–358. http://doi.org/10.1016/j.biopsych.2006.03.040

Jacobi, C., Hayward, C., de Zwaan, M., Kraemer, H. C., & Agras, W. S. (2004). Coming to terms with risk factors for eating disorders: Application of risk terminology and suggestions for a general taxonomy. *Psychological Bulletin, 130*(1), 19–65. http://doi.org/10.1037/0033-2909.130.1.19

Jewell, T., Collyer, H., Gardner, T., Tchanturia, K., Simic, M., Fonagy, P., & Eisler, I. (2016). Attachment and mentalization and their association with child and adolescent eating pathology: A systematic review. *International Journal of Eating Disorders, 49*(4), 354–373. https://doi.org/10.1002/eat.22473

Junne, F., Zipfel, S., Wild, B., Martus, P., Giel, K., Resmark, G., . . . Lowe, B. (2016). The relationship of body image with symptoms of depression and anxiety in patients with anorexia nervosa during outpatient psychotherapy: Results of the ANTOP study. *Psychotherapy, 53*(2), 141–151. https://doi.org/10.1037/pst0000064

Kaye, W. H., Bulik, C. M., Thornton, L., Barbarich, N., & Masters, K. (2004). Comorbidity of anxiety disorders with anorexia and bulimia nervosa. *American Journal of Psychiatry, 161*(12), 2215–2221. http://doi.org/10.1176/appi.ajp.161.12.2215

Kaye, W. H., Fudge, J. L., & Paulus, M. (2009). New insights into symptoms and neurocircuit function of anorexia nervosa. *Nature Reviews Neuroscience, 10*(8), 573–584. http://doi.org/10.1038/nrn2682

Keski-Rahkonen, A., Hoek, H. W., Susser, E. S., Linna, M. S., Sihvola, E., Raevuori, A., . . . Rissanen, A. (2007). Epidemiology and course of anorexia nervosa in the community. *American Journal of Psychiatry, 164*(8), 1259–1265. http://doi.org/10.1176/appi.ajp.2007.06081388

Keys, A., Brozek, J., Henschel, A., Mickelsen, O., & Taylor, H. L. (1950). *The biology of human starvation: Vol. 1–2.* Minneapolis, MN: University of Minnesota Press.

Kotler, L. A., Cohen, P., Davies, M., Pine, D. S., & Walsh, B. T. (2001). Longitudinal relationships between childhood, adolescent, and adult eating disorders. *Journal of the American Academy of Child and Adolescent Psychiatry, 40*(12), 1434–1440. http://doi.org/10.1097/00004583-200112000-00014

Krampen, G., & Wald, B. (2001). Short assessment procedures for formative evaluation and adaptive indication in general and differential psychotherapy and counseling: Session-related rating scales for individual psychotherapy and counseling. *Diagnostica, 47*(1), 43–50.

Lasègue, E.-C. (1873/1997). On hysterical anorexia (a). *Obesity Research, 5,* 492–497.

Leichsenring, F., & Schauenburg, H. (2014). Empirically supported methods of short-term psychodynamic therapy in depression – Towards an evidence-based unified protocol. *Journal of Affective Disorders, 169,* 128–143. http://doi.org/10.1016/j.jad.2014.08.007

Lilenfeld, L. R. R., Wonderlich, S., Riso, L. P., Crosby, R., & Mitchell, J. (2006). Eating disorders and personality: A methodological and empirical review. *Clinical Psychology Review, 26*(3), 299–320. http://doi.org/10.1016/j.cpr.2005.10.003

Lock, J., & Le Grange, D. (2012). *Treatment manual for anorexia nervosa: A family-based approach* (2nd ed.). New York, NY: Guilford Press.

Löwe, B., Zipfel, S., Buchholz, C., Dupont, Y., Reas, D. L., & Herzog, W. (2001). Long-term outcome of anorexia nervosa in a prospective 21-year follow-up study. *Psychological Medicine, 31*(5), 881–890. http://doi.org/10.1017/S003329170100407X

McCullough, L. (2003). *Treating affect phobia: A manual for short-term dynamic psychotherapy.* New York, NY: Guilford Press.

McIntosh, V. V. W., Jordan, J., Carter, F. A., Luty, S. E., McKenzie, J. M., Bulik, C. M., . . . Joyce, P. R. (2005). Three psychotherapies for anorexia nervosa: A randomized, controlled trial. *American Journal of Psychiatry, 162*(4), 741–747. http://doi.org/10.1176/appi.ajp.162.4.741

Midgley, N. (2013). *The New Library of Psychoanalysis Teaching Series: Vol. 7. Reading Anna Freud.* London, UK: Routledge.

National Institute for Health and Care Excellence. (2017). *Eating disorders: Recognition and treatment.* Retrieved from https://www.nice.org.uk/guidance/ng69/evidence

Operationalized Psychodynamic Diagnosis Task Force. (Ed.). (2008). *Operationalized psychodynamic diagnosis OPD-2: Manual of diagnosis and treatment planning.* Cambridge, MA: Hogrefe Publishing.

Orlinsky, D. E., Geller, J. D., Tarragona, M., & Farber, B. (1993). Patients' representations of psychotherapy: A new focus for psychodynamic research. *Journal of Consulting and Clinical Psychology, 61*(4), 596–610. http://doi.org/10.1037/0022-006X.61.4.596

Peñas-Lledó, E., Bulik, C. M., Lichtenstein, P., Larsson, H., & Baker, J. H. (2015). Risk for self-reported anorexia or bulimia nervosa based on drive for thinness and negative affect clusters/dimensions during adolescence: A three-year prospective study of the TChAD cohort. *International Journal of Eating Disorders, 48*(6), 692–699. https://doi.org/10.1002/eat.22431

Perkins, S. J., Keville, S., Schmidt, U., & Chalder, T. (2005). Eating disorders and irritable bowel syndrome: Is there a link? *Journal of Psychosomatic Research, 59*(2), 57–64. https://doi.org/10.1016/j.jpsychores.2004.04.375

Pike, K. M., Walsh, B. T., Vitousek, K., Wilson, G. T., & Bauer, J. (2003). Cognitive behavior therapy in the posthospitalization treatment of anorexia nervosa. *American Journal of Psychiatry, 160*(11), 2046–2049. http://doi.org/10.1176/appi.ajp.160.11.2046

Reich, G., Cierpka, M., & Becker, S. (2010). *Psychotherapy of eating disorders: Disease models and therapeutical practice* (3rd ed.). Stuttgart, Germany: Thieme.

Schauenburg, H., Friederich, H.-C., Wild, B., Zipfel, S., & Herzog, W. (2009). Focal psychodynmic psychotherapy of anorexia nervosa. *Psychotherapeut, 54*(4), 270–280. http://doi.org/10.1007/s00278-009-0668-4

Schmidt, U., Brown, A., McClelland, J., Glennon, D., & Mountford, V. A. (2016). Will a comprehensive, person-centered, team-based early intervention approach to first episode illness improve outcomes in eating disorders? *International Journal of Eating Disorders, 49*(4), 374–377. https://doi.org/10.1002/eat.22519

Schmidt, U., Magill, N., Renwick, B., Keyes, A., Kenyon, M., Dejong, H., . . . Landau, S. (2015). The Maudsley Outpatient Study of Treatments for Anorexia Nervosa and Related Conditions (MOSAIC): Comparison of the Maudsley Model of Anorexia Nervosa Treatment for Adults (MANTRA) with specialist supportive clinical management (SSCM) in outpatients with broadly defined anorexia nervosa: A randomized controlled trial. *Journal of Consulting and Clinical Psychology, 83*(4), 796–807. https://doi.org/10.1037/ccp0000019

Schmidt, U., Oldershaw, A., Jichi, F., Sternheim, L., Startup, H., McIntosh, V., . . . Treasure, J. (2012). Out-patient psychological therapies for adults with anorexia nervosa: Randomised controlled trial. *British Journal of Psychiatry, 201*(5), 392–399. http://doi.org/10.1192/bjp.bp.112.112078

Selvini-Palazzoli, M. (1996). *The Master Work Series. Self-starvation: From individual to family therapy in the treatment of anorexia nervosa.* New York, NY: Aronson.

Serpell, L., Treasure, J., Teasdale, J., & Sullivan, V. (1999). Anorexia nervosa: Friend or foe? *International Journal of Eating Disorders, 25*(2), 177–186.

Smink, F. R. E., van Hoeken, D., & Hoek, H. W. (2012). Epidemiology of eating disorders: Incidence, prevalence and mortality rates. *Current Psychiatry Reports, 14*(4), 406–414. http://doi.org/10.1007/s11920-012-0282-y

Schors, R., & Huber, D. (2003). Psychoanalytic thinking, cognitive-behaviour therapeutic acting? In W. Herzog, D. Munz, & H. Kächele (Eds.), *Eating Disorders: Therapy Guide and Psychodynamic Treatment Concepts* (2nd ed., pp. 60–81). Stuttgart, Germany: Schattauer.

Steinhausen, H.-C. (2002). The outcome of anorexia nervosa in the 20th century. *American Journal of Psychiatry, 159*(8), 1284–1293. http://doi.org/10.1176/appi.ajp.159.8.1284

Stuhldreher, N., Konnopka, A., Wild, B., Herzog, W., Zipfel, S., Löwe, B., & König, H.-H. (2012). Cost-of-illness studies and cost-effectiveness analyses in eating disorders: A systematic review. *International Journal of Eating Disorders, 45*(4), 476–491. http://doi.org/10.1002/eat.20977

Stuhldreher, N., Wild, B., König, H.-H., Konnopka, A., Zipfel, S., & Herzog, W. (2015). Determinants of direct and indirect costs in anorexia nervosa. *International Journal of Eating Disorders, 48*(1), 139–146. http://doi.org/10.1002/eat.22274

Summers, R. F., & Barber, J. P. (2012). *Psychodynamic therapy: A guide to evidence-based practice.* New York, NY: Guilford Press.

Teufel, M., Wild, B., Giel, K. E., Friederich, H.-C., Resmark, G., de Zwaan, M., . . . Junne, F. (2017). Family, partnership, education and occupation in patients with anorexia nervosa. *Psychotherapeut, 62*(3), 212–221. http://doi.org/10.1007/s00278-017-0194-8

Thomae, H. (1963). Some psychoanalytic observations on anorexia nervosa. *British Journal of Medical Psychology, 36,* 239–248. http://doi.org/10.1111/j.2044-8341.1963.tb01284.x

Thompson, A., Shaw, M., Harrison, G., Ho, D., Gunnell, D., & Verne, J. (2004). Patterns of hospital admission for adult psychiatric illness in England: Analysis of Hospital Episode Statistics data. *British Journal of Psychiatry, 185,* 334–341. http://doi.org/10.1192/bjp.185.4.334

Touyz, S., Le Grange, D., Lacey, H., Hay, P., Smith, R., Maguire, S., . . . Crosby, R. D. (2013). Treating severe and enduring anorexia nervosa: A randomized controlled trial. *Psychological Medicine, 43*(12), 2501–2511. http://doi.org/10.1017/S0033291713000949

Treasure, J., Claudino, A. M., & Zucker, N. (2010). Eating disorders. *Lancet, 375*(9714), 583–593. https://doi.org/10.1016/S0140-6736(09)61748-7

Troop, N. A., Allan, S., Treasure, J. L., & Katzman, M. (2003). Social comparison and submissive behaviour in eating disorder patients. *Psychology and Psychotherapy, 76*(Pt3), 237–249. http://doi.org/10.1348/147608303322362479

US Department of Agriculture and Department of Health and Human Sciences. (2015). *Dietary guidelines for Americans: 2015–2020.* Retrieved from http://health.gov/dietaryguidelines/2015/guidelines/

Vall, E., & Wade, T. D. (2015). Predictors of treatment outcome in individuals with eating disorders: A systematic review and meta-analysis. *International Journal of Eating Disorders, 48*(7), 946–971. http://doi.org/10.1002/eat.22411

Ward, A., Ramsay, R., Turnbull, S., Benedettini, M., & Treasure, J. (2000). Attachment patterns in eating disorders: Past in the present. *International Journal of Eating Disorders, 28*(4), 370–376. http://doi.org/10.1002/1098-108X(200012)28:4<370::AID-EAT4>3.0.CO;2-P

Wild, B., Friederich, H.-C., Gross, G., Teufel, M., Herzog, W., Giel, K. E., . . . Zipfel, S. (2009). The ANTOP study: Focal psychodynamic psychotherapy, cognitive-behavioural therapy, and treatment-as-usual in outpatients with anorexia nervosa – A randomized controlled trial. *Trials, 10,* 23. https://doi.org/10.1186/1745-6215-10-23

Wild, B., Friederich, H.-C., Zipfel, S., Resmark, G., Giel, K., Teufel, M., . . . Herzog, W. (2016). Predictors of outcomes in outpatients with anorexia nervosa: Results from the ANTOP study. *Psychiatry Research, 244,* 45–50. http://doi.org/10.1016/j.psychres.2016.07.002

World Health Organization. (1992). *International statistical classification of diseases and related health problems* (10th rev.). Geneva, Switzerland: Author.

World Health Organization. (2018). *International classification of diseases for mortality and morbidity statistics* (11th ed., stable version for implementation). Geneva, Switzerland: Author. Retrieved from https://icd.who.int/browse11/l-m/en

World Health Organization. (n.d.). *The ICD-10 classification of mental and behavioural disorders: Clinical descriptions and diagnostic guidelines* (pp.

138–139). Geneva, Switzerland: World Health Organization. Available from http://www.who.int/classifications/icd/en/bluebook.pdf?ua=1

Wu, M., Brockmeyer, T., Hartmann, M., Skunde, M., Herzog, W., & Friederich, H.-C. (2014). Set-shifting ability across the spectrum of eating disorders and in overweight and obesity: A systematic review and meta-analysis. *Psychological Medicine, 44*(16), 3365–3385. http://doi.org/10.1017/S0033291714000294

Zastrow, A., Kaiser, S., Stippich, C., Walther, S., Herzog, W., Tchanturia, K., . . . Friederich, H.-C. (2009). Neural correlates of impaired cognitive-behavioral flexibility in anorexia nervosa. *American Journal of Psychiatry, 166*(5), 608–616. http://doi.org/10.1176/appi.ajp.2008.08050775

Zeeck, A., Hartmann, A., Wild, B., de Zwaan, M., Herpertz, S., Burgmer, M., . . . Zipfel, S. (2016). How do patients with anorexia nervosa "process" psychotherapy between sessions? A comparison of cognitive-behavioral and psychodynamic interventions. *Psychotherapy Research,* 1–14. https://doi.org/10.1080/10503307.2016.1252866

Zipfel, S., Giel, K. E., Bulik, C. M., Hay, P., & Schmidt, U. (2015). Anorexia nervosa: Aetiology, assessment, and treatment. *Lancet Psychiatry, 2*(12), 1099–1111. http://doi.org/10.1016/S2215-0366(15)00356-9

Zipfel, S., Löwe, B., Reas, D. L., Deter, H. C., & Herzog, W. (2000). Long-term prognosis in anorexia nervosa: Lessons from a 21-year follow-up study. *Lancet, 355*(9205), 721–722. https://doi.org/10.1016/S0140-6736(99)05363-5

Zipfel, S., Seibel, M. J., Löwe, B., Beumont, P. J., Kasperk, C., & Herzog, W. (2001). Osteoporosis in eating disorders: A follow-up study of patients with anorexia and bulimia nervosa. *Journal of Clinical Endocrinology & Metabolism, 86*(11), 5227–5233. http://doi.org/10.1210/jcem.86.11.8050

Zipfel, S., Wild, B., Gross, G., Friederich, H.-C., Teufel, M., Schellberg, D., . . . Herzog, W. (2014). Focal psychodynamic therapy, cognitive behaviour therapy, and optimised treatment as usual in outpatients with anorexia nervosa (ANTOP study): Randomised controlled trial. *Lancet, 383*(9912), 127–137. https://doi.org/10.1016/S0140-6736(13)61746-8

8 Appendix: Tools and Resources

Nutrition Guidelines for Patients With Anorexia Nervosa

Dear Patient,
With the following guidelines, we would like to inform you about the general aspects of a balanced and healthy diet, as well as describing the specific noteworthy aspects of rebuilding nutrition after long periods of undernourishment and malnutrition. During the absorption of nourishment, the body not only receives energy, but is also supplied with micronutrients such as vitamins, minerals, trace elements, fiber, and secondary plant substances; all are indispensable to life. A regular, healthy, and balanced diet can be summed up with the questions, When, how, what, and how much am I eating?

1. When Do I Eat? (Building up a Regular Meal Plan)

The first step to normalizing your eating behavior is to reintroduce a regular meal structure. Based on the findings to metabolism processes, after eating and during phases of hunger, it is advantageous for a healthy adult to have periods of at least 2 hrs between meals but no longer than 6–7 hrs. Taking this into account along with portion size, the recommendation is that adults eat between three and six meals a day.

What does this mean for me as a patient with anorexia nervosa?
Since patients with anorexia nervosa generally prefer smaller portions at the beginning of their recovery, the approach in clinical practice has crystallized as having three main meals along with two snacks and an additional late meal, which has proven most sensible.

A regular meal structure of six meals per day
The recommendation of more frequent, though smaller meals than those suggested for a healthy adult applies to anorexic patients who experience problems when ingesting the size of food portions recommended or for whom, for instance, weight gain remains illusive.

If required: a regular meal structure of nine meals per day

2. What and How Much Do I Eat? (Nutrition Components and Portion Size)

Information on the nutritional composition of foods and recommended portion sizes takes into account common choices of food and nutritional habits. As these differ worldwide from country to country, food-based dietary recommendations are given by national associations and ministries. Following, the US guidelines are presented in detail, which can serve you as a good orientation and can be adapted if necessary for country-specific recommendations.

From: H.-C. Friederich, B. Wild, S. Zipfel, H. Schauenburg, & W. Herzog: *Anorexia Nervosa* © 2019 Hogrefe Publishing

The nutrition guidelines for a wholesome diet (including eating and drinking for healthy adults) are presented by the US Department of Agriculture and Department of Health and Human Sciences in their *Dietary Guidelines for Americans 2015–2020* (USDA and HHS, 2015).

For the purposes of graphic illustration, the individual food groups are presented on a plate, with the size of each segment representing the recommended portion size. For each meal, fruits and vegetables should cover half of the plate; grains, grain products, and potatoes, one quarter; and food containing protein, the remaining quarter. The meal is completed with a further portion of dairy products (http://www.choosemyplate.gov/).

The basis for this visual representation was the Healthy US-Style Eating Patterns, one of three USDA Food Patterns that are used as examples translated into the recommended and specific quantities of the food groups (USDA and HHS, 2015). As foods within any one food group differ to a greater or lesser extent regarding the levels of energy and nutrient density, cup equivalents (c-eq) and ounce equivalents (oz-eq) have been introduced to make the foods comparable with respect to their nutritional content. The presented amounts (detailed recommendations for healthy adults) describe the target portion sizes and frequencies with which you should consume the respective food groups.

You should consume 2.5 c-eq/day of the food group vegetables and 2 c-eq/day of the food group fruits. It should be noted that 1 c-eq is 1 cup of raw or cooked vegetables or fruit, 1 cup of vegetables or fruit juice, 2 cups of leafy salad greens, one-half cup dried fruit or vegetables. With these foods, a large proportion of your daily requirements of vitamins, minerals, trace elements, and fiber are supplied. As foods within this food group show great differences regarding their level of nutritional density, you should consider varying your selection, as well as alternating between leaving the fruits and vegetables raw or cooked. On the bases of the different nutritional densities of the vegetables, specific recommendations are given for the five vegetable subgroups that relate to the intake during 1 week: dark green vegetables 1.5 c-eq/week, red and orange vegetables 5.5 c-eq/week, legumes (beans and peas) 1.5 c-eq/week, starchy vegetables 5 c-eq/week, and other vegetables 4 c-eq/week.

Of the grains group, 6 oz-eq/day should be consumed. This food group comprises grains as single foods (e.g., rice, oatmeal, and popcorn), as well as products that include grains as an ingredient (e.g., breads, cereals, crackers, and pasta). Grains are either whole or refined. As the nutritional content of whole grains and refined grain products differ, particularly for iron and fiber, it is recommended that you consume at least half of your grains as whole grains (whole grains ≥ 3 oz-eq/day, refined grains ≤ 3 oz-eq/ day). One oz-eq corresponds to one-half cup of cooked rice, pasta, or cereal; 1 ounce of dry pasta or rice; 1 medium (1 ounce) slice of bread; 1 ounce of ready-to-eat cereal (about 1 cup of flaked cereal).

Of the protein foods, 5.5 oz-eq/day are recommended. Similar to vegetables, subgroups are used that provide an orientation for the quantities over 1 week. Animal protein includes the subgroups seafood (8 oz-eq/week) as well as meats, poultry, eggs (26 oz-eq/week); vegetable protein is found in the subgroups nuts, seeds, and soy products

From: H.-C. Friederich, B. Wild, S. Zipfel, H. Schauenburg, & W. Herzog: *Anorexia Nervosa* © 2019 Hogrefe Publishing

(5 oz-eq/week). Examples for 1 oz-eq are 1 ounce of lean meat, poultry, or seafood; 1 egg; one-quarter cup of cooked beans or tofu; 1 tablespoon peanut butter; one-half ounce nuts or seeds.

Because legumes have a similar nutrient profile to foods containing protein as well as vegetables, to meet the recommended intake levels, they can be considered either a vegetable or a protein food. Green peas and green (string) beans are not counted in the legume subgroup, because their nutrient composition is not similar to legumes. Green peas are similar to starchy vegetables and are grouped together with onions, iceberg lettuce, celery, and cabbage in a vegetable subgroup.

If you would like to refrain from eating meat or fish, then you can meet your protein needs with a clever combination of dairy protein or eggs and plant protein. Popular dishes in this category are, for example, wholegrain bread with cheese, a casserole of macaroni and cheese, boiled potatoes with a Greek yogurt herb dip, mashed potatoes made with milk, skillet potatoes covered in egg, cereals with milk or yogurt, bean chili served with bread or over rice, and lentils made with noodles or rice. The recommendations for a vegetarian diet are 3 oz-eq/week of eggs, 6 oz-eq/week of legumes (beans and peas in addition to 1.5 c-eq of the vegetables group), 8 oz-eq/week of soy products, and 7 oz-eq/week of nuts and seeds.

Of the dairy food group, including milk, yogurt, cheese, and fortified soy beverages (i.e., soymilk), one should eat 3 c-eq/day. Examples of 1 c-eq are 1 cup of milk, yogurt, or fortified soymilk; 1.5 ounces of natural cheese such as cheddar cheese or 2 ounces of processed cheese.

As soy beverages are enriched with calcium and vitamin A and D, they are very similar to milk in nutritional content, in contrast to other plant-based "milk beverages" (e.g., almond milk, rice milk, coconut milk) – they are part of the dairy food group.

Since you, unlike a majority of the adult population, do not have a high body weight, you should choose meat, fish, and egg products, and milk and milk products with their natural fat percentage. This is contrary to what the USDA recommends for a healthy adult diet. Choosing these non-reduced-fat or "normal" products will help you gain the needed weight to place you in the normal weight range by eating regular portion sizes.

Oils deliver essential life-sustaining fatty acids and vitamin E, and should be added to the meal daily in quantities of 5 teaspoons.

In order to meet the recommendations for nutritional intake within a balanced energy intake, it is important to rely on natural, unprocessed foods. Once these recommended amounts are realized in a healthy diet, a small amount of energy needs (about 10–15%) to maintain body weight are still not yet covered by the described eating guidelines. The USDA Food Patterns indicate that these calories are "limits on calories for other uses" (USDA and HHS, 2015). Thus, it is possible within the context of recommendations for a healthy eating style to also recommend the moderate consumption of sweets, salty snacks, and sweetened drinks. Foods from this group are not, per se, damaging to health or prohibited. They should, however, be used as an indulgence and

From: H.-C. Friederich, B. Wild, S. Zipfel, H. Schauenburg, & W. Herzog: *Anorexia Nervosa* © 2019 Hogrefe Publishing

not as a source of nutrients. And since indulgence is defined by moderate consumption, we recommend eating portions of this food group regularly (USDA and HHS, 2015).

What do these recommendations mean for me as a patient with anorexia nervosa?

The above-mentioned recommendations describe portion size goals and the frequency with which foods belonging to the different food groups should be eaten. Due to your anorexia nervosa and its accompanying symptoms, you should pay special attention to the following:

- Regular intake of grain products and potatoes to normalize the hunger-satiation regulation system
- Regular intake of high calcium foods like whole milk, milk products, and high calcium mineral water to strengthen bones
- Meat, milk, and milk products with their natural fat levels, to facilitate normalizing weight gain while eating normal adult portions
- An adequate supply of protein through meat, fish, or effective vegetarian combinations (milk protein and egg in combination with vegetable sources of protein), to help strengthen muscles
- Fats in a normal serving size, preferably plant oils to supply all necessary fatty acids and fat-soluble vitamins.

If you choose to follow a vegetarian meal plan, then an ovo-lacto-vegetable combination is suggested so that milk, milk products, and eggs are consumed. With this meal plan, it is generally possible to supply your body with all life-sustaining nutrients.

Particular Specifics After Long-Term Fasting or Laxative Use

Patients who retain a body mass index (BMI) of ≥ 15 kg/m^2 can usually reinstate a balanced intake of nutrients without complications. A careful increase in the consumption of nutrients is not medically necessary. However, the prolonged fasting and misuse of laxatives can cause changes to the intestinal membranes that may result in indigestion. For this reason, as well as for psychological reasons, we recommend that patients increase their food intake step by step and avoid foods prone to causing indigestion during the first 2 weeks. Furthermore, a secondary lactose deficiency (the enzyme responsible for breaking down lactose) can cause intolerance to milk and other milk products. This enzyme deficiency can be reversed as the intestinal membranes recover enabling the increased digestion of milk products with time.

A general recommendation is that patients begin with an intake of about 1,500 kcal and increase their intake gradually. In the long run, the ingestion of 1,500 kcal will not suffice for adequate weight gain. To reach the weight gain goal of 500 g/week the intake of nutrients must be increased to 3,000 kcal (these numerical specifications are meant to provide a general orientation; individual variations are possible). The necessary energy intake that will create weight gain can be consumed in the normal portion sizes during the recommended six to eight meals, spaced throughout the day. For this reason, it is unnecessary to consume high-calorie drinks, though in certain exceptions the consulting doctor may advise their temporary use.

From: H.-C. Friederich, B. Wild, S. Zipfel, H. Schauenburg, & W. Herzog: *Anorexia Nervosa* © 2019 Hogrefe Publishing

What does this recommendation mean for me as a patient with anorexia nervosa?

After long-term fasting or prolonged abuse of laxatives you should:

- keep to a regular meal structure comprising 6–8 meals;
- eat easily digested foods and milk products low in lactose;
- increase step-by-step energy intake in the first few weeks.

In the following we provide two examples of a daily plan from which one can project the nutrient composition and portion size of meals.

Example 1: Daily Plan for the First Weeks After Prolonged Fasting

Time of day	Meals
8:00 a.m. breakfast	1 piece of whole-wheat bread 1 tsp butter/margarine (80% fat) 1 tbsp cottage cheese (20% fat) 2 tsp marmalade 1 glass of fruit juice
10:00 a.m. 1st snack	1 fruit yogurt (200-g container, 3.5% fat) 1 piece of fruit (apple, pear, banana)
12 noon lunch	1 dessert bowl of salad 1 tbsp vegetable oil 1 tsp vinegar 1/2 cup rice (measured dry) 2 bell peppers 60 g turkey breast 1 ladle of gravy/curry sauce
3:30 p.m. 2nd snack	1 fruit yogurt (200-g container, 3.5% fat)
7 p.m. dinner	1 piece of whole-wheat bread 1 tsp butter/margarine 1 piece of cheese (45% in the dry matter) 2 tomatoes
9:30 p.m. Bed-time snack	2 pieces of chocolate (about 10 g)
Balance	Energy: about 1,500 kcal Carbohydrates: about 206 g (56 E%) Protein: about 54 g (15 E%) Fats: about 48 g (29 E%)

Note. tsp = teaspoon, tbsp = tablespoon, E% = % of daily energy supply

Example 2: After the Step-by-Step Increase in Nutrient Intake

Time of day	Meals
8:00 a.m. breakfast	1 piece of whole-wheat bread 1 tsp butter/margarine (80% fat) 1 tbsp cottage cheese (20% fat) 2 tsp jam 6 tbsp of cereal/muesli 7 fl oz milk (3.5% fat) 1 glass of fruit juice
10:00 a.m. 1st snack	1 piece of whole-wheat toast 1 tsp butter/margarine (80% fat) 1 piece of cheese or deli meat 1 piece of fruit (apple, pear, banana)
12 noon lunch	1 dessert bowl of salad 1 tbsp vegetable oil 1 tsp vinegar 3/4 cup rice (measured dry) 2 bell peppers 150 g of turkey breast 2 ladles of gravy/curry sauce
3:30 p.m. 2nd snack	1 piece of bunt cake 1 glass of fruit juice
7:00 p.m. dinner	2.5 pieces of whole-wheat bread 3 tsp butter/margarine (80% fat) 3 tsp Greek yogurt with fresh herbs (40% fat) 1 piece of cheese (45% in the dry matter) 2 tomatoes 1 glass of tomato juice
9:30 p.m. Bed-time snack	1 candy bar (e.g., Milky Way) 20 soft candies (e.g., gummi bears)
Balance	Energy: about 3,000 kcal Carbohydrates: about 406 g (55 E%) Protein: about 110 g (15 E%) Fats: about 99 g (29 E%)

Note. tsp = teaspoon, tbsp = tablespoon, E% = % of daily energy supply

3. Taste and Enjoyment

In addition, variety in taste influences the biochemical processes that regulate hunger and satiation in a positive manner. That said, all sensory perceptions are in fact of importance. Besides the five different basic gustatory tastes (sweetness, saltiness,

From: H.-C. Friedrich, B. Wild, S. Zipfel, H. Schauenburg, & W. Herzog: *Anorexia Nervosa* © 2019 Hogrefe Publishing sourness, bitterness, savouriness), tactile perception (consistency, surface texture, temperature, spiciness), the sight and the odour of food as well as the sound heard when biting into food, for example into an apple, fresh rolls, or crisps, all affect our appetite.

Even though our preference for sweet tastes and our aversion to bitter tastes are innate and can be best explained from an evolutionary perspective, these preferences are subject to variation over the course of life, i.e., if and in which concentration these taste perceptions are experienced as pleasant (taste is also always trainable).

In order to taste and enjoy food, a variety in flavors and reasonable time intervals are necessary. You will achieve variety by following the recommendations on individual food groups and diet composition listed in Sections 1 and 2 above. With regards when to eat, it is important to be aware that both fast and prolonged periods of eating prevent you realizing how much you have eaten and may also trigger binge-eating attacks. In practice, we have found that allowing 10 minutes for a snack or small late meal and about 30 minutes for a main meal is beneficial.

What does this mean for me as a patient with anorexia nervosa?

To taste and enjoy your meals, we recommend:

- a varied and balanced diet
- ca. 30 minutes for a main meal
- ca. 10 minutes for a snack or small late meal

Acknowledgments

We would like to thank Sandra Schild for her contributions to these Nutrition Guidelines.

From: H.-C. Friederich, B. Wild, S. Zipfel, H. Schauenburg, & W. Herzog: *Anorexia Nervosa* © 2019 Hogrefe Publishing

Weight Curve

How to Use the Weight Curve

The weight curve helps the patient and therapist to monitor the client's body weight during the course of treatment. This appendix provides a blank weight curve and a sample completed weight curve. Weighing should take place weekly before the therapy sessions.

The body weight in lb is entered on the y axis and the week of treatment on the x axis. The solid lines on the y axis represent increments of 2 lb and the dotted lines increments of 0.5 lb. The solid lines on the x axis represent each week of treatment (Week 1 to Week 40).

The individual body weight of the patient at the beginning of treatment should be entered as a whole number without decimals on the y axis (see *) and at the "0" position on the x axis. This baseline can be highlighted by drawing a line across all 40 weeks (see completed weight curve). The body weight of the sample patient at the beginning of treatment was 92.5 lb and is therefore recorded as 92 lb. The following data should then be inserted for each week with an accuracy of 0.5 lb on the dotted or solid vertical lines (see again the sample weight curve).

From: H.-C. Friederich, B. Wild, S. Zipfel, H. Schauenburg, & W. Herzog: *Anorexia Nervosa* © 2019 Hogrefe Publishing

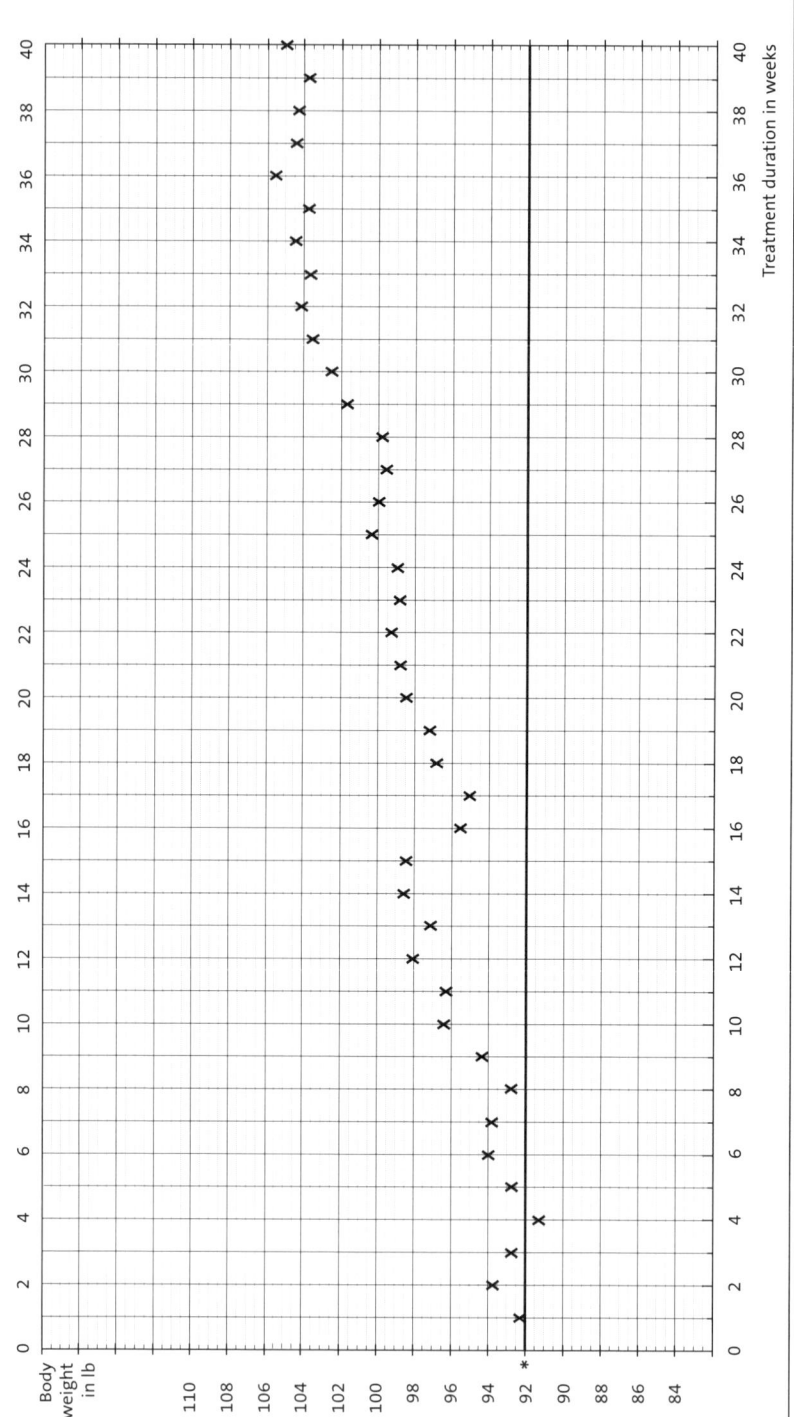

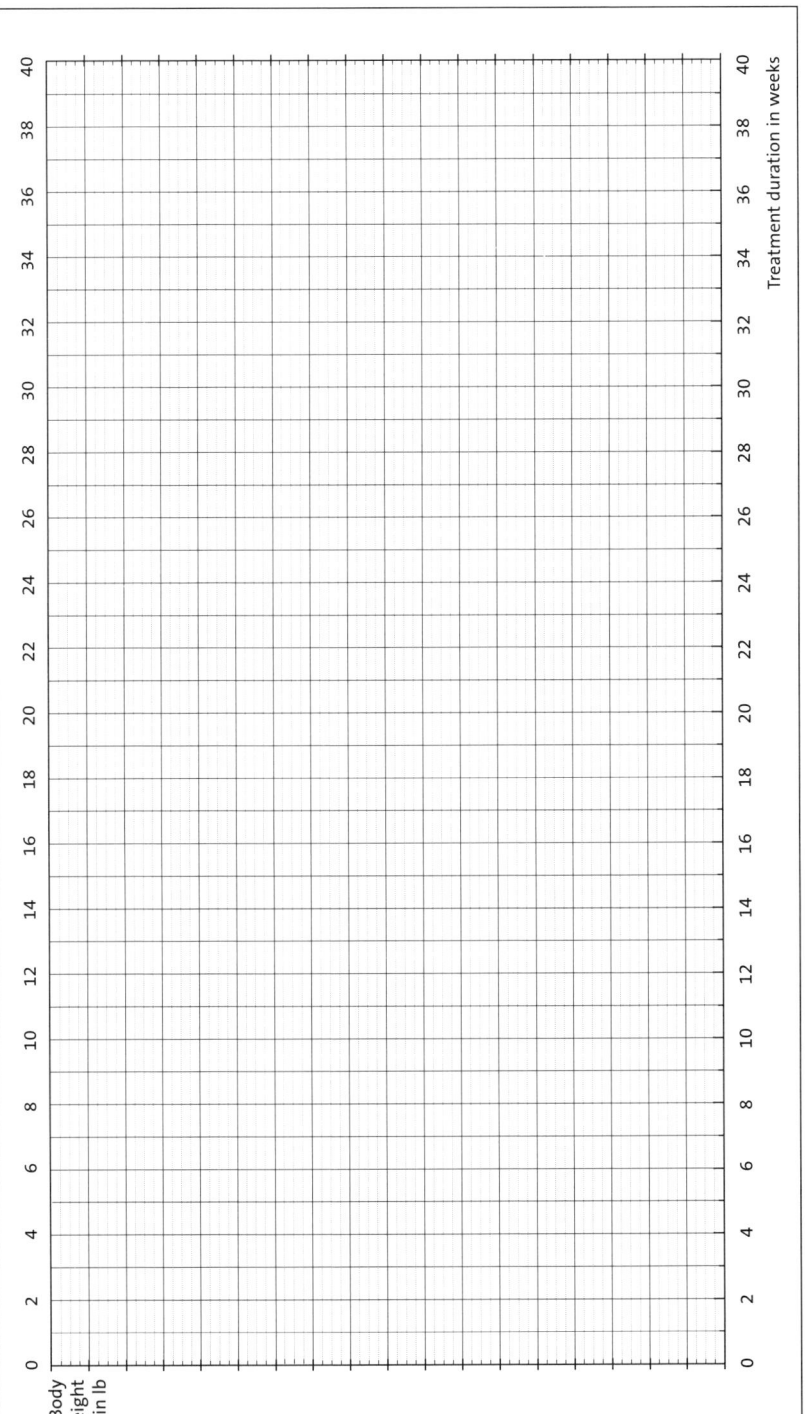

Body weight in lb

Treatment duration in weeks

Note: y axis: solid horizontal lines represent an increment of two lb, dotted horizontal lines represent an increment of 0.5 lb.
Please enter body weight at the beginning of treatment as a whole number in lb without decimal places as shown in the sample weigth curve.
Insert the treatment week the body weight was taken (x axis) with the weight measured below and above the baseline weigt to an accuracy of 0.5 lb (y axis).

This page may be reproduced by the purchaser for personal/clinical use.
From: H.-C. Friederich, B. Wild, S. Zipfel, H. Schauenburg, & W. Herzog: *Anorexia Nervosa*

© 2019 Hogrefe Publishing

Contributors

Hans-Christoph Friederich
Psychosomatic Medicine and Psychotherapy
University Düsseldorf
Moorenstr. 5
40225 Düsseldorf
Germany
hcfriederich@online.de

Wolfgang Herzog
General Internal Medicine and Psychosomatics
University Hospital Heidelberg
Im Neuenheimer Feld 410
69120 Heidelberg
Germany
wolfgang.herzog@med.uni-heidelberg.de

Miriam Komo-Lang
General Internal Medicine and Psychosomatics
University Hospital Heidelberg
Thibautstr. 2
69115 Heidelberg
Germany
miriam.komo@med.uni-heidelberg.de

Henning Schauenburg
General Internal Medicine and Psychosomatics
University Hospital Heidelberg
Thibautstr. 2
69115 Heidelberg
Germany
henning.schauenburg@med.uni-heidelberg.de

Sandra Schild
Psychosomatic Medicine and Psychotherapy
University Hospital Tübingen
Osianderstraße 5
72076 Tübingen
Germany
Sandra.schild@med.uni-tuebingen.de

Beate Wild
General Internal Medicine and Psychosomatics
University Hospital Heidelberg
Im Neuenheimer Feld 410
69120 Heidelberg
Germany
beate.wild@med.uni-heidelberg.de

Stephan Zipfel
Psychosomatic Medicine and Psychotherapy
University Hospital Tübingen
Osianderstraße 5
72076 Tübingen
Germany
stephan.zipfel@med.uni-tuebingen.de

The multiaxial diagnostic system based on psychodynamic principles, now for children and adolescents

OPD-CA-2 Task Force / Franz Resch /
Georg Romer / Klaus Schmeck /
Inge Seiffge-Krenke (Eds.)

OPD-CA-2
Operationalized Psycho-
dynamic Diagnosis in
Childhood and
Adolescence

Theoretical Basis and User Manual

2017, xvi + 334 pp.
US $69.00 / € 54.95
ISBN 978-0-88937-489-8

Following the success of the Operationalized Psychodynamic Diagnosis for Adults (OPD-2), this multiaxial diagnostic and classification system based on psychodynamic principles has now been adapted for children and adolescents by combining psychodynamic, developmental, and clinical psychiatric perspectives.

The OPD-CA-2 is based on four axes that are aligned with the new dimensional approach in the DSM-5: I = interpersonal relations, II = conflict, III = structure, and IV = prerequisites for treatment. After an initial interview, the clinician (or researcher) can evaluate the patient's psychodynamics according to these axes to get a comprehensive psychodynamic view of the patient. Easy-to-use checklists and evaluation forms are provided. The set of tools and procedures the OPD-CA-2 manual provides have been widely used for assessing indications for therapy, treatment planning, and measuring change, as well as providing information for parental work.

www.hogrefe.com